The Spiritual Hedonist

A guide to the Divine art and practice of living joyfully

"This is the purpose of life—to get what you want. There are deeper things, but this is fun."
Karl Lagerfeld

Sheilaa Hite, CLC, C.Ht.

©2017

Pictorial Muses photos © 2012 by Franciscus van der Werf

Author's photo, front cover by Lyndie Benson
Author's photo, back cover by Stephanie Stanton,
www.stephaniestantonphotography.com

Published by The Center for Practical Spirituality

Printed in the United States of America

ISBN 978-0-9916-5532-8

The Center for Practical Spirituality
P.O. Box 472
Lenox, MA 01240 USA

www.SheilaaHite.com

I dedicate this book to all of the dreamers—
the "Somewhere Over the Rainbow" kindred spirits—who really
do want their dreams to come true.

~ ~ ~

"Unless it is supported by a practical plan,
no creative, mundane or spiritual concept
can come to successful fruition."

— Sheilaa Hite

Contents

"Both quantum physics and metaphysical thought affirm that we create our reality by our intentions."
—Sheilaa Hite

Acknowledgements

Acknowledging people and thanking them for their contributions is one of my favorite things to do. I'm happy to be able to do that here for the people who were there for me and who helped make it possible for me to get my message out to the world.

In the early stages of writing *The Spiritual Hedonist*, I suffered from what seemed to be an insurmountable and impenetrable bout of writer's block when my colleague, friend and advisor, Dr. Janice Seward, came to my rescue. She wouldn't take 'no' for an answer and gently, firmly guided me to the major break-through that got me back on track with finishing this book. Without her belief in me and her calm, supportive insistence that I keep at it, this book would still be on my 'I'll finish it one day' list.

After Dr. Janice Seward, the next people I let read it were author and editor, Winslow Eliot and editor Ginny Guenette. They had nothing but praise for the book and encouragement for me and it was Ginny who suggested I use one of my favorite expressions, *The Spiritual Hedonist*, as the title. I will be forever thankful to them for their expertise, generosity and support.

Winslow, as a writer, could see where I was getting bogged down energetically, and intuitively knew just the right thing to say to help me continue to move through whatever resistances cropped up for me. Winslow, as my editor, put the finishing touches on *The Spiritual Hedonist* and helped me present my new creation to the world.

I am blessed to have so many supportive friends who see and love my light. Their encouragement is and has been invaluable in living my truth, as well as writing this book.

I thank David Nathan, singer, songwriter, music journalist, author and seer, for his unflagging support, wonderful friendship and writing advice.

A happy expression of gratitude to my website designer, Tom Stier of PromoteGlobally.com, for creating an on-line system for displaying the Pictorial Muses.

I am infinitely grateful to and encouraged by those who continue to amaze me with their creative capacity for experiencing life to the fullest; Franciscus van der Werf, for the use of his wonderful photographs that became my Pictorial Muses, Frances T. Matlock, teacher extraordinaire, who made it her life's work to guide her students to their greatness, the wonderful Lena Horne who insisted that I see and treasure my light, Karl Lagerfeld, philosopher and creative genius whose 'Life' quote continues to inspire all of us, Venus Rachal, James Wecker II, Casy and Richard Cann-Figel, Maurice Peterson, Jeriann Griffith, Charles Drayman, Cassandra Saulter, Delores Banks, Floyd Banks and all of the way-showers and role models who've gone before me.

With all my heart, I thank my guardian angel, my maternal grandmother, Lois. I love you and I'm so blessed to have you with me. Forever and ever, I thank you for watching over me. I feel your love and your wings around me always.

And, as always, I thank the "Front Office"—God—my source, my inspiration, my reason for being.

Preface

What is a Spiritual Hedonist?

"I believe that the very purpose of our life is to seek happiness. That is clear. Whether one believes in religion or not, whether one believes in this religion or that religion, we all are seeking something better in life. So, I think, the very motion of our life is towards happiness."

–Dalai Lama

T hat's blasphemy!" shouted the fellow tourist I'd encountered in Rome. "How can you be spiritual and a Hedonist at the same time? Isn't hedonism a bad thing and doesn't being spiritual mean to live in a sacred way?"

As she shouted these words at me, I had to suppress a laugh—we were on the rooftop terrace of a beautiful 5-star hotel that overlooked the Eternal City. The late October temperature was balmy and the light breeze felt like a caress as it gently stroked my skin. She was reclined "Empress style" on a chaise lounge, eating fruit at ten o'clock at night and enjoying a glass of proseco—Italy's wonderful homage to champagne.

She didn't realize it, but this tourist was at that very moment embodying many of the essential principles of a Spiritual Hedonist. She was drinking Italy's delicious answer to champagne, proseco, on that hotel terrace that balmy night in Rome because a few days before, she'd decided to give herself a treat for no other reason than she wanted to.

She was married, owned her own business and sat on the board of directors of the company that she had founded, and her children were grown and off on their own.

She'd taken a few days away from the office for some much needed pampering and relaxation at her local spa. She'd made the sudden decision to spend those few days in Italy instead, because she had realized that even though the relaxing spa near her New England home would do, it would be so much more beneficial and fun to combine the relaxing spa experience with the ancient civilization, site-seeing, great restaurants, fabulous shopping experience. In other words, she was in Rome having a good time and taking care of herself because it made her feel good (and on some level, she knew she deserved it).

She'd asked her husband to accompany her, but he was off to a golf camp that week, so she called a friend and even though it was short notice and they didn't have a "real reason" (organized tour, anniversary, work, illness, etc.) to go—they realized they didn't have a real reason not to go, either. Their only purposes for the trip were experiencing pure pleasure and feeding their souls.

Because they were enjoying treating themselves well, they felt better about themselves and their lives. This invigorated them and they radiated genuine good feelings, which were reflected back to them by all of the people they'd met on this trip. They knew that when they returned home they'd feel so much better and their world would reflect their good feelings, too.

When I began to explain what Spiritual Hedonism is and to point out how they were exemplifying that, they realized that what I was telling them wasn't separate from their spiritual lives, it was an intrinsic part of their spirituality and added to the richness of their spiritual and mundane experiences. "Oh," said the 'Empress,' *"so being good to myself and generous to myself and enjoying the process is a spiritual thing to do. Well, I guess hedonism isn't such a bad thing after all when you look at it that way."* Her friend agreed and we all lifted our glasses and toasted their new awareness and our new-found fellowship with a sip of the Italian nectar of the gods.

So, what did I say to the 'Empress' and her friend on that rooftop terrace in Rome that instantly shifted their perspective and dissolved their resistance to the idea of Spiritual Hedonism and being a Spiritual Hedonist?

I simply told them the truth. I told them the truth in a way that they could hear it with their ears, hearts and souls. I began by directing their attention to a source that we can all relate to and rely on—Webster's Dictionary.

The word, *spiritual* is an adjective whose root word is the noun *spirit*. *Spirit* is defined by Webster's dictionary thusly; *the animating principal of life; vital essence; the soul or heart as the seat of feelings; a vigorous, courageous or optimistic attitude; an individual as characterized by a particular attitude; a dominant tendency or character; God; to encourage; ardor, vigor, zeal.*

Webster defines the adjective *spiritual* as, *of or pertaining to sacred things or matters; pertaining to or consisting of spirit; pertaining to the spirit or soul.*

Hedonism is a word that comes from the Greek and is defined as *the doctrine that pleasure and happiness are the highest good* and a hedonist is defined as someone who enjoys life and takes pleasure in living. In other words, a hedonist is really someone who lives their life wanting and seeking to enjoy life and the process of living in the most spiritually practical way.

A Spiritual Hedonist is someone who walks their own sacred path—a unique blend of what is personally sacred and meaningful to them and what is collectively sacred and meaningful to the world at large. A Spiritual Hedonist is one who pursues their own 'personal legend,' and by doing so, discovers and reconnects with Divine Source, their own Divine birthright and the path of joy.

Unfortunately, as a society, we've forgotten how to walk that path, or even where it is or how to find it.

Sadly, the very intense reaction of the "Empress" to the term, Spiritual Hedonist, is not that unusual. The combination of those two words—Spiritual and Hedonist—really pushes buttons with a lot of people. When an objection is raised, it's about the word 'hedonist' used in connection with the word, 'spiritual.' Many people seem to think that those two words used together—Spiritual Hedonist—cancel each other out.

Up until the last few years of the previous century, as far as common thought was concerned, one could either be considered spiritual <u>or</u> a hedonist—one couldn't be both. There was little or no realization that the two could be combined into one entity or life path and there was certainly no awareness that the word, 'spiritual,' could be used as an adjective to define or clarify the term, 'hedonism.'

Fortunately, in today's world, we've grown and continue to grow beyond the narrow confines of many old definitions, including the one generally used for the word 'hedonist.'

The first time the phrase, Spiritual Hedonist, came into my mind, I was on the down escalator in the department store, Galleries Lafayette, in Paris. Galleries Lafayette is like a giant toy/treasure chest filled with all of the things that speak to your soul that you didn't know existed until you saw them. It's like an adult version of the magical toy store in the wonderful film, "Mr. Magorium's Wonder Emporium." More than once, a shopper radiant with unbridled child-like joy, turned to me holding onto their new find and exclaimed, *"Can you believe it!? I've never seen things like this!"*

I knew what they were talking about. I'd felt it too, even before I walked into the store. That store and what I could find there were the impetus for adding a stop in Paris to my European business trip itinerary. Two months before, I'd met a woman who was wearing the most fabulous sunglasses I'd ever seen. They were beyond description. My soul cried out for them. She told me she'd gotten them at Galleries Lafayette in Paris. Though I'd never heard of the store, I knew I had to go to Paris and get those glasses.

The store's escalators open to the entire ground floor of the store. As I stood on the descending escalator, I could see everything happening on the main floor below me. As I watched in wondrous awe, the customers, like the kids in "Mr. Magorium's Wonder Emporium," shopped with a joy and a sense of abandon and a camaraderie I'd never seen anywhere else. It wasn't a store full of strangers; it was a community of life's happy celebrants sharing in the bliss of the experience of the moment.

That's when the phrase, *"The Spiritual Hedonist,"* moved from my heart and into my mind. My experience of being in Galleries Lafayette that day was truly a spiritual experience and it was hedonism at its finest. In that moment of clarity, I knew I was to write this book.

It was an experience I'm grateful for and will never forget. It was so impactful that it wasn't until I was back in my Parisian friend's apartment showing him all of my newly acquired treasures, that I realized with a shock, that I'd totally forgotten something. He looked at all of my new purchases and asked, *"Well, where are the sunglasses, did you find them?"* It wasn't until that moment that I realized that my whole reason for being in Paris—those fabulous sunglasses—had been completely erased from my soul as soon as I'd walked into that wonderful treasure emporium on Haussmann Boulevard! Once inside the store, I never thought about them. It wasn't until my next trip to Paris that I, with the help of another friend, returned to Galleries Lafayette and found my own version of those wonderful sunglasses.

Of course I would have this awakening in Paris, the most visited city in the world! That's what Paris is and why we love it—it's the personification of Spiritual Hedonism at its best.

If the true definition of hedonism is that living a life of joy is the highest good and being spiritual means more than being pious, self-sacrificing or reclusive, how did society come to believe that these two words indicate something that is bad, evil, selfish or negative?

The denotation or actual meaning of a word is often set aside by parties who benefit from substituting their own definition for the word. Once the actual meaning of the word is substituted for a meaning that a particular group approves of, the new meaning (the connotation) is used and advocated by the benefitting parties.

The fault lies in the misidentification of the connotation of the words 'spiritual' and 'hedonist' as the denotation. The belief that hedonism or hedonists are bad, evil, selfish, immoral or negative, comes from labels that have come into use since Western society, prompted by organized religion during medieval times, began to suppress anything that related to feeling good. This suppression not only related to the primal sensual self, it also related to just about everything that would make a person feel anything other than guilt (especially about wanting to feel good about themselves or experiencing personal happiness).

The belief that one needs to sacrifice one's personal feelings, live their lives from an all-consuming sense of duty to everyone and everything other than oneself and/or make amends for wanting/needing to be happy is the actual culprit here. This belief, promoted by those in positions of power, was used to control others and attain their physical, spiritual and psychological assets.

Those controlled by this belief system are programmed to believe that wanting to live a life filled with joy and experience personal satisfaction is selfish, immoral and wrong and pursuing these natural inclinations will consign them to everlasting damnation. They were and continue to be programmed to suppress these positive, natural, healthy feelings about themselves and life at every possible turn in exchange for a promise that all that they were suppressing or denying themselves would be available to them in an afterlife paradise.

Several years ago, a man named Rev. Ike emerged from society's shadows of guilt and self-denial. He was a very popular, positive thinking, charismatic minister, televangelist, visionary (and by definition, a Spiritual Hedonist) named Reverend Ike (Rev. Frederick J. Eikeronkoetter II). He gained an international following when he famously exhorted his listeners to stop thinking they had to wait until they died and went to Heaven to get their reward for a well lived life. He insisted that it was everyone's birthright to live a joy filled, prosperous life as he encouraged them to *"Forget about the pie-in-the-sky when you die; get yours here and now."*

Most people adored him because he told them the truth about their birthright of deservability and freedom from want. He taught them to look within and see that the Divine Force wanted them to be happy and successful. His followers prospered monetarily, emotionally and spiritually.

It is a sad historical fact that some people love or identify with their misery so much that they get very upset when anyone steps forward and insists on living his or her life in an abundant, joy-filled manner. Rev. Ike's stance ignited a firestorm of criticism from his detractors—*"How could he be a man of God and not believe in suffering and lack?"* *"Who was he to think that it was of the highest spiritual good to enjoy life and all of the positive joyfulness it offers?"*

Rev. Ike didn't let that stop him from delivering the powerful, positive messages of his ministry. He and the members of his world-wide congregation continued to prosper and enjoy their lives. They let the results of their beliefs and actions provide the proof that the nay-sayers demanded. They consciously created their own reality and so can you.

Anyone who ever had a dream and worked to make it come true is a Spiritual Hedonist. From Christopher Columbus, Thomas Edison, Amelia Earhart, Leonardo da Vinci, modern-day role models, to us—we are all Spiritual Hedonists!

Have you ever helped someone or done even the smallest kindness for someone because it not only helped them, it made you feel good or happy or connected in some way to humanity or all of life? In other words, did interacting in and with life give you pleasure? If your answer is yes, you've already stepped over the line—you are a Spiritual Hedonist

"But that's different!" some of you out there may be saying. "*I did that because...*" or "*I felt good because...*" You can end those sentences with any of a number of excuses or reasons, but the bottom line is, if you helped or extended yourself for another person, entity or cause and you did so because it made you feel good or you realized afterward that feeling good was a by-product or an added benefit of your kind act, you fit the Webster's dictionary definition of (a) Spiritual—adj.—*as, of or pertaining to sacred things or matters; pertaining to or consisting of spirit; pertaining to the spirit or soul; of or pertaining to the soul as the seat of moral or religious nature.* And (b) Hedonist—n.—*a person who practices the doctrine that pleasure or happiness is the highest good.*

Children are great examples of Spiritual Hedonists. They genuinely, naturally express the pure joy that has its home in their hearts. Without artifice or self-condemnation, they live in a joyful state of just being naturally who and what they are and asking for and expecting to get what they want. And they remain that way until they're forced to comply with society's limiting belief systems that their birthright, life's limitless supply of joy and abundance, is in short supply and must be conserved at all costs.

The Spiritual Hedonist is a person who has awakened from the programmed nightmare of denial, self-abnegation and intentional or unnecessary suffering. They no longer need instructions or permission from society on how and what to feel and think because they have at last given themselves permission to think for themselves and to be fully engaged in and enjoy their lives. They are fully alive and know that every moment is a moment to be experienced, to be lived to the fullest.

The Spiritual Hedonist is, by nature, a moral person, concerned with experiencing and interacting with life in a mutually beneficial, balanced and ethical manner, with this very important distinction, they just don't have being moral, ethical and balanced confused with being miserable, evil or deprived. They joyfully conduct their life in such a way that their thoughts, feelings and actions contribute to the well-being of the world as a whole as well as themselves.

A Spiritual Hedonist is also a generous and caring person—they just remember to give to and care for and about themselves, too. They have re-connected to their hearts—the center of joy, passion, desire, innocence and love in all ways, including spiritually, creatively and romantically. The heart is the place where Divinity lives. It doesn't matter what Divinity means to you or what form Divinity takes—from the most reverent of us to the most atheistic of us—what is personally Divine to us is what gives meaning to our lives and dwells in the holiest place of all—the heart.

This book, this philosophy, this espousal will definitely ruffle some feathers, rattle a few nerves and be considered seditious by those who are uncomfortable with the idea of enjoying living a personally satisfying life. These people were taught and still cling to the limiting, false belief that life is suffering, and that redemption is only possible through pain and loss or by enduring some horrible personal sacrifice, and that our 'joy' will come to us only after we die. They slavishly hold onto the fallacy that only an outward form of salvation, i.e., someone else proclaiming their worth/value or bestowing some type of 'grace' upon them, gives them and their life any real meaning.

It's true that life can be painful and difficult at times. Sometimes we do and must endure some type of suffering and we are occasionally called upon to sacrifice something dear to us for the greater good, or worse, for no apparent reason.

But these incidents are not a way of life, a reason for living or proof of any kind that we must live in an unfulfilled manner, and they are not meant to be. They are some of the circumstances that we, as souls who are having a human experience, encounter and must deal with appropriately in the process of evolving and living. They do not define us, our path, our way of engaging with or experiencing life. They do not define us as a people, a species, as souls or as spirit.

That is not Divine or natural intention for us—to endlessly and needlessly suffer and live our lives in denial and pain. We are meant to be happy and the Divine and natural intention for us is to live meaningful, joy-filled, productive lives.

This book is an instruction manual and a road map. Consider reading and working with it a journey home to your true essence. Enjoy the adventure!

Introduction

T his is the purpose of life—to get what you want. There are deeper
things, but this is fun. When I first read those words, my
heart felt like it had just received the kind of life restoring
energy jolt that's administered to a cardiac arrest patient by an
Emergency Room doctor.

In that moment, I was alive in a way I'd never been before and I
knew it. Karl Lagerfeld's quote worked as a defibrillator and
reawakened my passion for life as it restored my connection to the
knowledge that, with the appropriate awareness, attitudes and
actions, anything is possible.

At the time I came across his quote, I was teaching a life
enhancement class in Malibu, California. It was a popular class and
both my students and I loved it. I was teaching others how to live at
their maximum best, yet I was floundering. My life felt stagnant and
whatever I did, I couldn't seem to make any headway in stimulating
my career and enhancing my own life. Through it all though, I
maintained a positive attitude and prayed for the miracle that
would deliver the golden goose of prosperity and stability to me.

The miracle came from a direction I'd never have expected (but
that's the nature of miracles, isn't it?). One evening, while talking
on the phone with a friend who was also one of the students in my
enhancement class, she asked me what my aspirations were and
what I was doing to make them happen. I replied, "Oh,—I'm doing my
guided imagery CD's. I'm really good at leading people through the guided
imagery process and everyone who hears them tells me how powerful and
effective they are. My plan is to promote them in such a way that they
introduce and attract more clients to me."

We continued talking about the things that good friends talk
about with each other—life, love, shopping and the state of the
world.

The next day, Saturday, she called and invited me to dinner the
following night—her treat. She's a very fiscally conservative person,

i.e., "tight-fisted" with money, who rarely treats anyone to anything. I knew then, that she had something on her mind and it was important that we get together over dinner. I also liked spending time with her, so I happily accepted. We decided on where and when for our meal and just before we hung up, she said, *"Oh, bring a notebook with you."*

When I heard those words, that little butterfly flutter that goes through your stomach when something's about to happen, went through mine. *"Uh-oh,"* I thought, *"something's up."*

At the restaurant that evening, after we'd ordered our entrees and while we were sipping our drinks, hers—Malbec wine; mine—champagne, she asked me again about my aspirations and what I was doing to make them happen. I replied, *"I'm doing my guided imagery CD's; you know how much everybody likes my guided imagery meditations."*

And that's when she said something that completely changed my perspective—*"You've been saying that for quite some time. Tell me, where are you recording them, what studio are you using? How much are blank CD's in bulk? Who's going to reproduce and package them?"*

I realized, with a shock, that I had no answers to her questions! Once I'd decided to record my guided imagery meditations, in my mind, that's what I was doing. I wasn't consciously aware of the fact that, while I was busy producing my CD's in my head, I wasn't doing anything on the material plane to manifest them as physical entities. The concept was good; I just hadn't followed through on it with actions that would produce concrete results!

And that's when it hit me—that's what we human beings do! We experience the rush of an inspiration or an idea and, "high" on the fumes of that rush, we viscerally live out all of the possible permutations of it, and if we do that long enough, instead of applying actions that will actually lead to and produce what we're dreaming of, we come to believe that we're doing something that's going to show up here, in the physical realm.

That moment was one of the single most pivotal moments in my life. Once I consciously realized what I'd been doing, I very clearly got what needed to be done—not just by me, but by every one of us who dreams of something more for ourselves and then suffers the disappointment of not having those dreams come true. All of our lives, we're told that we can have and be anything we can dream of, but for most of us, no one explained exactly how. Since no one issued us an instruction manual explaining what manifestation is, how it works and how to work it, we've struggled to make our dreams a reality and way too often have failed at physically creating what our hearts can so clearly see.

Over a period of time, the disappointments from all of those accumulated failed dreams morph into a kind of resignation and hopelessness that deafens us to the message our hearts have never stopped trying to get through to us, that we have a birthright, spiritually, physically and emotionally to live a grace filled, joyous life.

I saw all of that in that moment and it made for very lively dinner conversation that evening. I never took any notes—I didn't have to. It was all so clear. I knew what I had to do and I knew that I was going to do it to my benefit as well as to the benefit of my students and anyone else who wanted to live the joyful, productive life they were meant to.

I went home that evening and began working with the miracle I'd been granted. As I worked, I realized that achievement is a ten-step process and those ten steps are grouped into four levels of development or stages of completion. Each stage represents a level of accomplishment, marking your progress as you work toward the manifestation of your goal.

I began to see that all creation stems from the combined correct balance of feminine and masculine energies. Manifestation (converting the infinite into the finite) is actually the physical form of Spirituality. I call it and the action required to bring it about "the fourth leg of Spirituality" because they represent the fourth stabilizing leg or element of the life supporting platform of Spirituality; the energies of all four of the elements must be present, balanced and working together in order to bring anything into being. Those four elements are spirit or inspiration, heart or passion, mind or development and ability or appropriate action.

The first three elements are ethereal and very important and necessary to any endeavor. You can be inspired to create, have passion for your inspiration and make great plans to develop it, but if you don't apply the fourth element—appropriate, timely action, all you'll ever have is an ethereal result—"castles in the air." That's what the great philosopher, Henry David Thoreau, was referring to when he said, *"If you have built castles in the air, your work need not be lost; that is where they should be. Now put foundations under them."* The castle's supportive foundation can only be built with the appropriate, physical actions.

Simply put, meaningful manifestation can only be achieved by taking timely and appropriate physical action and applying it to your inspired, desired, planned for goals. The physical manifestation of anything represents how you're focusing your energy and consciously or unconsciously using it. If you want to know what you're committed to, just look at what keeps happening in your life.

At the next class session the following Tuesday, I introduced my new manifestation creation system. I announced to the class that we'd all be doing this exercise in creating what we wanted. I called it, "How to Turn Lead Into Gold," and I described it as modern-day alchemy—the art, magic and miracle of transformation. Alchemy is the ancient art of turning base metal—your dream, vision, wish or idea, into gold—the physical manifestation of those ethereal unformed energies.

The response was electric! It was as though they'd been waiting for me to present them with this opportunity. Each one of my students knew immediately what dream they wanted to bring into being. The outward form of each quest was different; they ranged the gamut from one person wanting to learn to grow orchids all the way to one woman who, though she'd been married for ten years, wanted to remedy the fact that she'd never met her in-laws or her husband's teen-age children from his previous marriage. The inner desire was the same for all of us, though, we wanted to end our involuntary confinement in the realm of disappointment and broken dreams. And, yes, we all achieved our dream, some in only a couple of weeks and some took a little longer, but we all had the liberating experience of pursuing and attaining an important goal.

Since that time, I've continued to work with and develop this system of achieving success no matter what your goal is. Over the years, I've worked with and taught it to thousands of people who've successfully used this system to achieve their goals and make their dreams come true. I know what to do, why it's important, how it all fits into the pattern or plan and I know and understand the dynamics of successfully working that plan to bring an inspiration, an idea, a dream to fruition.

We do live in interesting times. Almost everything we were once certain of has changed and we must change with it. We're a success driven, goal oriented culture. We thrive on big dreams, big plans, big wins. That's part of what defines us as a society. Without having and manifesting a vision of who you are and who you want to be, you won't be able to grow, spiritually or emotionally, and you'll never be able to feel the satisfaction of knowing your life's purpose—to make the world a better place because you were here and to enjoy the journey in the process.

Now is the perfect time for this book and the perfect time for you to be reading it because the new frontiers that we're encountering call for a different method of exploration and development. These interesting times also call for the explorer—you—to engage with the energy of the moment and align yourself with the forward moving trajectory of 21st century life.

The persistent, consistent, committed actions you take will make all the difference in whether you win or lose as you pursue your goals. Your focused, determined actions are the bridges that will take you successfully through the valleys, the highs, the rough and the smooth terrains of your process-journey to completion and success.

This undeniable truth is beautifully put by the 30th president of the United States, Calvin Coolidge:

> "Nothing in the world can take the place of persistence.
> Talent will not—
> nothing is more common than unsuccessful men with talent.
> Genius will not—
> unrewarded genius is almost a proverb.
> Education will not—the world is full of educated derelicts.
> Persistence, Determination and Faith alone are omnipotent."

It's important to keep in mind, that your actions always determine the outcome of anything and your *right* actions always determine a successful outcome.

The first three steps of successful manifestation are the most important. They are the steps that will ensure that you have all that you require in order to establish a solid foundation for the successful completion of your project. These first three steps are the "gathering" steps and are often energy and time intensive because of their thoroughness. The thoroughness of this first stage of completion is necessary to your success and is reflected in the depth, length and scope of chapters one, two and three. Remember, as in all things, the value of the attention—time and energy—you put into preparing your foundation is priceless and always, ultimately rewarding. To paraphrase the wisdom of legendary UCLA basketball coach, John Wooden, *"Failing to prepare is preparing to fail."*

As you work with my system of creating success, you'll be actively engaging with your vision and miracles will happen. Expect them by allowing circumstances to provide them to you. Accept them by being aware that a miracle has presented itself to you. And receive them by welcoming them in and making them a part of your manifestation process.

You're reading this book because you have a vision, a dream, an ideal that you want to bring into being. It's the "gift that keeps on giving." Throughout this book, you'll meet people just like yourself, who worked with this system and made their dreams come true. If you follow the directions laid out for you here, you will achieve success, too.

As you continue to read, pay attention to what pushes your buttons, what causes a negative or painful thought or emotion. At those places, ask yourself, *"Who installed those buttons and where did that reaction come from?"* And then, listen for the memories, thoughts and feelings that come up for you. You'll start to become conscious of the source of limiting belief systems and old programming.

Notice, too, what makes you smile or what feels right and natural to you. At those times and places, you're experiencing a conscious connection to your soul's true identity. Acknowledge those occurrences and celebrate your discovery of another aspect of what makes you unique and blessed.

All you need now is a system that works—a step-by-step system that will bring everything together and guide you as you make it all happen. That step-by-step system is here in your hands right now. This book is the result of my soul's quest to obtain those precious jewels that make life meaningful—living happily, unconditionally loving myself and showing others that they can live the same way. By presenting this success system to you, I gladly offer you its guidance, wisdom and power. I don't know what you'll create or how you'll transform your life by using this "instruction manual." I do know that you will discover your true magnificence and connection to the infinite power of your essential self as you embark on and participate in one of the most rewarding adventures of your life—getting, having and enjoying what you want.

May All Your Dreams Come True!

Before We Begin...

The Pictorial Muses

The old adage, "*A picture is worth a thousand words,*" is as true today as it was when those words were first spoken. We are a visual species and what we see can evoke thoughts, feelings and memories that consciously connect us to meaningful experiences and essential truths that are personal and unique to each of us.

Every successful creative venture is inspired and encouraged by a muse—a dynamic source of inspiration. The photos and the words of the *Pictorial Muses* will act as those dynamic sources of inspiration for you as you work to make your hopes, wishes and dreams a reality. By working with these pictorial muses, you'll be able to more easily and consciously access previously hidden information, realizations and intuitive support that will be of great help to you as you take the steps necessary to manifest your desire.

Choosing the Three Pictorial Muse Images that will describe you and your quest

1. Go to my website, www.SheilaaHite.com, and click on *The Spiritual Hedonist* link. When the page opens, set your intention by taking three deep, rhythmic, gentle breaths and then, click on the **Pictorial Muse Images** link. The three images that will describe you and your quest will appear. Write the word that appears with each image in your journal. Write your impression of each word and its accompanying image and what thoughts and/or feelings come up for you when you look at it. The three images and words that have come up for you are a reflection of you, your combined strengths and your best qualities as you

work with this manifestation process. Every time you see or think of them, you'll be activating the part of your brain that allows you access between your conscious and subconscious mind.

Print the page out and place it in a notebook where you can refer to the images on a regular basis. You can also display the printed page of your images on a bulletin board.

Choosing the Four Pictorial Muse Images that will identify the key energy of each stage

2. Next, again set your intention by taking three deep, rhythmic, gentle breaths and then click on the *Four Pictorial Muse Images* link on the *Three Pictorial Muse Images* page. The four images that will identify the key energy of each of the four stages of your manifestation journey will appear. Going counter clockwise, the image that represents Stage 1 is the top left image. The image that represents Stage 2 is the top right image. The image that represents Stage 3 is below the Stage 2 image and the image that represents Stage 4 is to the left of the Stage 3 image. Write the word that appears with each image in your journal. Write your impression of each word and its accompanying image and what thoughts and/or feelings come up for you when you look at it. Each of the four images and words that have come up for you identifies the key energy that resonates for you in that particular phase of the manifestation process. In each stage of the process, the image and word you've chosen for it will act as a prompt for your psyche, allowing you to access and utilize the important knowledge hidden in your subconscious mind.

Print the page out and place it in a notebook where you can refer to the images on a regular basis. You can also display the printed page of your images on a bulletin board.

Note: If you choose one of these four images when you're picking your *Daily Pictorial Muse Image*, the events of that day will have a special, more impactful meaning to you.

Choosing the Daily Pictorial Muse Images that will inspire and empower you on your quest

3. At the start of each day, go to my website, www.SheilaaHite.com, and click on the *Spiritual Hedonist* link. When the page opens, set your intention by taking three deep, rhythmic, gentle breaths and then click on the **Daily Pictorial Muse Images link.** Your image for that day will appear. Write the word that appears with the daily image in your journal. Write your impression of the word and its accompanying image and what thoughts and/or feelings come up for you when you look at it. Your **Daily Pictorial Muse Image** will identify the core energy that resonates for you and reflects your energetic focus for the day. Pay attention to any intuitive feelings you get about a particular person, idea or circumstance.

At the end of the day, look at your **Daily Pictorial Muse Image** again. Notice what your impressions are now and if your thoughts and/or feelings about the image have changed. Notice how the image's word, picture or your impression of it showed up for you during the day. Write your second impression of your **Daily Pictorial Muse Image** in your journal immediately following your earlier noted impressions.

Print the page out and place it in a notebook where you can easily refer to it on a regular basis. You can also display the printed page of the day's image on a bulletin board.

Guided Imagery Meditations

The power of guided imagery meditations can't be overstated. They're great for assisting you in accessing and exploring your inner consciousness. These guided imagery meditations were specifically designed to be used with this manifestation process. They will help you establish and maintain a relationship with your process and your goals by enhancing and strengthening your connection to them as well as providing support for you during your journey to the actual manifestation of what was once only a vision, dream, hope or wish.

With a "Treasure Map", you'll use photographs or drawings to represent your vision and what it means to you. Photos of your dream in physical form are a great reminder and every time you look at it, something in your psyche declares ownership of it. By working with it you're subconsciously helping to bring your vision into physical form. Instructions for creating your own "Treasure Map" can be found in the appendix section at the back of this book.

Work Book Exercises

I recommend that you make copies of the Work Book Exercises pages at the end of each chapter and keep them together in a notebook. I also recommend that you do the exercises by hand. Although writing by hand means you'll be recording information the old fashioned way, it's still the most powerful way to begin and support the process of manifestation.

Journaling

In addition to the Work Book Exercises, I also recommend that you get a journal in which to further record your experiences. This very pivotal time in your life will be filled with many new awareness's, feelings and thoughts. The transformation and birth of the "new" you will be rich, profound and different from anything you've experienced before and you'll want to document *it*.

On Procrastination

Procrastination is another word for self-denial. By avoiding or resisting beginning (or in some cases, completing) the steps to finish a project, you deny yourself the knowledge, experience and proof that you're a winner; that you *can* make your dreams come true.

When you say to yourself, *"I'm too tired when I get home,"* or *"I have so much on my plate, I can't make room for that now,"* or any variation of my personal favorite–*"I'll do it tomorrow, or after the sports season, or after my favorite TV show or* _____ *(you fill in the blank),"* you're really saying, *"I don't believe in myself or my dream enough to put any effort into it. Sure, I want it, but can't it just magically appear?"*

It would be great if your dream could just magically appear, but it won't. Making your dream come true requires a kind of discipline that demands that you focus your desire, attention and energy on taking and completing the steps that will bring you to the successful completion of your goal.

You're never too tired when you're inspired. You don't always begin each session or task inspired, though. Sometimes you have to "fake it 'til you make it." Start working on the task at hand and you'll discover that you've gotten so involved in it and so inspired by what you're doing that you've completely forgotten about being tired or missing that game or TV show.

If you've got too much on your plate, it's time to take an honest look at what you're committing your time and energy to. Do you have an hour or 30 minutes or even 15 minutes a day to focus on your goal? Then, commit that time on a constant basis, however much it is, to working on some aspect of the successful outcome of your dream. After a while, you'll find that more time and energy will become available to you. It'll just happen. But first, you do have to commit the time and take the right steps.

The Importance of Listening to Your Intuition

Intuition, sometimes called hunches, is your greatest, most powerful ally in any endeavor. It's a direct message to you from "the Front Office"—God, Higher Power, Divine Spirit. Learn to listen for it and to it as you work to manifest your goal. It can point you in the right direction and confirm the information you've gotten by using logic and intellect.

How can you tell the difference between your intuition giving you information and your mind just chattering? The messages your intuition delivers come through in a calm, unemotional, almost matter-of-fact way, while the mind chatter tends to express itself in a heightened emotional manner—it shouts, cries, is afraid and/or is hysterical.

The information your intuition gives you is never wrong, while the information your mind chatter delivers is often biased and/or misleading. By listening to the downloaded Guided Imagery meditations that come with this book, you'll be able to develop and better trust a deeper level of more insightful intuition.

Chapter 1

The number "1" is an inspiration number.
It's the number that relates to beginnings and new ideas and
visions, to inspirations, dreams and desires as well as enthusiasm for
those ideas and visions.

**This is the most important chapter in this book. It will teach you
how to know exactly what you want, so that you'll be able to get
exactly what you want.**

*"Take care to get what you like
or you will be forced to like what you get."*
—George Bernard Shaw

Yo quiero–Io voglio–I want. No matter what language you
speak–these are the most important words you need to say
in order to begin the process of conscious creating.

Did you know that at any given time, we are never more than
two hours away from the process of manifesting our desired reality?

Creating, manifesting or obtaining anything always starts by
your being able to ask and answer the question—*What do I want?*
And getting or attracting the necessary valuable assistance you'll
need starts with being able to answer this variation of the same
question—*What do you want?*

You're reading this book because you *do* want something
that's important to you and you want help getting it. So, I ask you,
what do you want to create, bring into being or manifest?

Sounds simple doesn't it? And it is. Your answer needs to be
specific, though. It amazes me how indirect we can be when it
comes to stating our wants and desires. Whether we're talking to

others or speaking to our hearts, we seem to be determined to perfect the art of "beating around the bush" or telling ourselves or others why an important wish can't become a reality, i.e., *"It costs a lot of money to open a restaurant,"* or *"Everyone tells me that there are too many day spas already,"* or *"Artists can't support themselves,"* or _____(fill in your own reason).

Whenever I ask that question—*What do you want?*—whether to an individual client or a group of attendees at a seminar, the majority of answers go something like this: *"Happiness," "To make a lot of money," "To be safe and secure," "To meet someone"* and a perennial favorite—*"I don't know."*

When I hear, *"Happiness," "To make a lot of money," "To be safe and secure," "To meet someone"* or *"I don't know,"* I bring their attention to a couple of important points.

Point 1: with the exception of not knowing what they want, the *"I"* is missing from their statements. And if the *"I"* is missing when they talk about what's important to them, it's missing from their hearts, their minds and their lives, as well. Point 2: they need to be specific about what they want if they are going to be successful in achieving their goals.

Until that moment, most of them aren't even aware that they're being vague about themselves and what really matters to them.

As a society, we've learned to skirt around or avoid altogether our personal involvement in what's really important to us. Somewhere along the way, we bought into an old Puritan belief that we are committing a wrong if we speak directly about ourselves as individuals, especially if it's about something we want.

"I" is defined in Webster's dictionary as the <u>1-</u> *nominative singular pronoun used by a person in referring to herself or himself* and <u>2-</u> *the self.* The personal pronoun, *"I,"* is a very important word. Without it, we wouldn't be able to think or talk about ourselves as individuals and we wouldn't be able to differentiate between others and ourselves. We wouldn't be able to personally label what is or isn't important to us and we wouldn't be able to direct the energy to ourselves when we attempt to get our needs met or when we want to communicate to others what is important to us.

"*I*" is the power word in any request or statement. It carries the vigor of your life force because it refers to and identifies YOU. When you leave it out of a request or statement, it's energetically the same as photo shopping your face out of a picture—you aren't there, you don't count, you are null and void. And if you're null and void, you're not likely to be a powerful magnate, able to purposely, consciously attract your good, are you?

Begin listening to yourself whenever you think or talk about what you want. Notice how often "*I*" is left off when you refer to yourself, from the simplest thought to the most desired objects. Notice how you feel when you do that. And notice how you feel when you use "*I*," how just referring to yourself in that straightforward manner gives you a feeling of power and presence.

Being specific means being precise or detailed and it's a key element in having clear, understandable communications with others and yourself. When you're not specific, confusion, frustration and dissatisfaction are the result.

I'll illustrate my point by using this analogy: you go to a restaurant with a sign in the front window that reads, "*Breakfast served all day.*" The waiter comes to your table to take your order. You tell him you want eggs. The waiter asks you how many eggs and how you want them prepared. You reply, "*You know, eggs—you work here and you serve breakfast all day, you should know what I want.*"

The waiter goes to the kitchen and returns with a plate of eggs. You look at them and see that there are only two of them and they're over easy, and you don't like your eggs over easy. You tell the waiter that he got it wrong. He repeats his original question to you, "*How many eggs do you want and how would you like them prepared?*" You again tell him that you don't know and since he serves breakfast all day, he should know what his customers are looking for in a good breakfast. At this point, both you and the waiter are frustrated. You're hungry, you aren't being fed and you can't get what you want. And he can't do his job, which is to make sure he delivers what you really want, once he knows what that is.

The restaurant represents life. It has everything you want and need to feel satisfied. The waiter represents the Universe, waiting to take your order so that it can provide you with whatever you want.

And the eggs, well, the eggs represent the physical manifestation of what you want. They represent what will sustain, support and satisfy you.

Life is like a restaurant with a vast and varied menu. Whatever you want is on it, but you do have to ask for it and you have to be specific, otherwise you're very likely to be unhappy, frustrated and dissatisfied with the results you get.

Yes, occasionally both you and "the waiter" get lucky and he guesses correctly and you get what you want on the first one or two tries. And with that method, that's what you're leaving your happiness up to—luck and guesses. There's no guarantee that your luck will hold out and there's no guarantee that you'll get exactly what you want and there's no guarantee you can duplicate your success.

There is great power in being specific. When I hear, *"Happiness," "To make a lot of money," "To be safe and secure,"* or *"To meet someone"* as an answer to the question, *"What do you want?"* I ask the person a series of questions that will help them become clear and specific about their desire.

The conversation goes something like this:

Me: *What do you want?*

Client: *"To meet someone."*

Me: *"Just anyone? You've met several people today, is that what you mean?"*

Client: *"No, someone I can be in a relationship with."*

Me: *"OK. There are a lot of different kinds of relationships—romantic, platonic, professional, spiritual, casual, serious—the list goes on. What kind of relationship are you talking about?"*

Client: *"Oh, I get it now. I want a serious, romantic relationship with someone who is available and who wants to be with me and who is compatible with me."*

Me: *"Great! Do you see how your original generic request—'To meet someone' differs from your specific request—' I want a serious, romantic* relationship with someone who is available and who wants to be with me and who is compatible with me.' Now we can take the steps necessary to put your order in to the Universe."

Or this:

Me: "What do you want?"

Client: "I want to make a lot of money."

Me: "What amount is a lot of money to you?"

Client: "Enough so that I can quit my job and move to Thailand. It's been my dream to live there and open an import-export business."

Me: "That sounds exciting! What kind of import-export business do you want to open and where in Thailand do you want to live?"

Client: "I haven't decided yet."

Me: "How much will it cost to open an import-export business and what are the regulations for operating a business in Thailand?"

Client: "I'm sure it'll cost a lot of money. I'll find out about the regulations once I move there and start working on my business."

Me: "How much is the airfare to Thailand and how long does it take to fly there?"

Client: "I don't know."

Me: "It's wonderful that you have a dream and you want to fulfill it. Before you can put your order in to the Universe, though, you need to do your part and do some research in order to find out what the specifics are in regards to your achieving your goal. Until you do, your goal will most likely remain an unfulfilled dream or become a failed one because you haven't gotten all of the information you'll need in order to sustain a move, a new business and a new life."

"It's better to be prepared for an opportunity that never happens, than to be unprepared for one that does."

—Les Brown

Suppose you're like a great many people I meet who ask the question, *"What if I don't know what I want?"* In truth, everyone knows what they want. Every one. The answer lies in your heart and the heart is where all of our wants and desires come from. The heart is like a five year-old child. It wants because it feels good to want whatever pleases it. Ask a five year-old what they want. Their answer will be something like this—*"I want an I-pod and a pony and an ice cream cone and a monster truck and..."* Now ask them what they want to be. *"Umm, I want to be an astronaut and a ballerina and a doctor and an acrobat and the President and..."* They usually have quite a list and they can go on for some time.

When you were five years old, you knew what you wanted and what you wanted to be, too. You didn't know you couldn't do, be or have those things until some adult, in an attempt to socialize you and save you from life's disappointments if you tried and failed to get what you wanted, recounted some version of their *"limitation litany."*

You know what a *"limitation litany"* is, don't you? It's that series of negative, self-limiting, discouraging beliefs that people use to explain why something can't or shouldn't be attempted or done. Do any of these sound familiar?

- *"In our family, we don't do that"*
- *"Girls (or boys) can't do that"*
- *"That's impossible—nobody can do that"*
- *"You want too much"*
- *"Stop daydreaming and be realistic"*
- *"You can't make a living doing that—you'll starve"*
- *"You're just kidding yourself—grow up!"*
- *"Do you think money grows on trees?"*
- *"Who do you think you are?"*

And lest we forget, let's reach back into the archives for a few "golden oldies":

- *"Stop dreaming of heart transplants, Dr. Barnard, they can't be done."*

- *"You can't attach wings to a tube, put people in it, and expect it to fly—it's impossible."*

- *"Everyone knows that the Earth is flat, Chris. You'll fall off the edge if you sail too far."*

- *"That's ridiculous—there's no way a telephone will ever be as small as a credit card."*

The list goes on and on.

It seems that every family and every society has some favorite self-limiting phrases that they nurture with their energy and the pain of their failed attempts to make their dreams come true. They lovingly guard these *"limitation litanies"* and with great solemnity, they carefully pass them on to every member of each succeeding generation, just like a valuable legacy.

These "most valuable" legacies are the reasons they cite when they explain their lack of achievements, their disappointments and their refusal to do anything to change their unfulfilling circumstances. They feel it's their duty to instruct and remind you of them often in order to protect you from the pain of possible failure if you have the audacity to buck the established trend and decide to go for it and make your dream come true.

For the most part, these "family treasures" are passed on as an act of love with no maliciousness intended. Handed down to you with 'mother's milk,' these "treasures" became encoded in your psyche and you unknowingly allowed them to act as your internal GPS, guiding you to failure whenever your soul's desires got the best of your "training" and you set out to make the impossible, both possible and real for you.

Now, please keep in mind that in most cases, your primary care givers socialization process wasn't done to harm you. When it's done in a gentle way and with a consideration for the individual uniqueness of the character of the child, it can help the child learn how to process their inner thoughts, feelings and desires so that they can translate and communicate them clearly and be understood by the world around them. And once clearly understood by self and by others, the child knows they are deserving and they become a powerful magnet for getting their hopes, wishes, needs and desires met.

Another method of squelching your dream faculty comes in the form of the *"Why?"* and *"Because"* indoctrination.

You're about five years old. You realize you want something and you go to your parents (or whatever caregivers you're with) and with great, innocent, childlike enthusiasm, you announce your desire. What do your parents respond with? *"Why?"* The first few times this happens, you're confused. After a while, though, you start to catch on. You begin to understand that their *"Why?"* is part of a code system that, if deciphered correctly, will get you what you want. You soon learn that the correct response begins with the magic word, *"Because."*

Ahh—*"Because."* You've been with your caregivers long enough to know that the word, *"Because,"* is always followed by an explanation that makes certain results seem possible or appropriate. This explanation is called a *"reason."* You search your five-year old memory and watch their reactions for your cues as you begin to recite what you've come to recognize as *"reasons."* Through this trial and error process, you discover the *"reasons"* —often called, *"good reasons"*–that please your caregivers and cause them to unlock the treasure chest and give you what you want.

In this process, you quickly discover that your real reasons, which come from your heart, are not good enough. *"I want it,"* *"It makes me feel good,"* *"I just do,"* won't cut it. You need a different form of currency if you're going to get what you want. Fortunately, your parents are willing to help you solve this riddle. When you respond with your truth—*" I want it,"* *"It makes me feel good,"* *" I just do,"*—they explain that that isn't enough, that you can't just want something; you have to have an acceptable (to them) reason for wanting it.

They then proceed to instruct and enlighten you in the proper way to bargain for your heart's desire. You learn the proper (to them) words and phrases that need to follow the lead or "key" word, "*Because.*"

Every parent has her or his own particular phrases that have meaning to them. Although they may be phrased differently, they're pretty much conveyed along these lines:

- "*It'll help me learn to be more responsible*"

- "*It'll be for my sister (or brother), too, and we can both learn to share*"

- "*It'll make me a better player for my team*"

- "*I'll learn how to handle money better*"

- "*I've been good all day and I deserve a reward*"

- "*I can wear the new clothes to several special events and that'll save you money*"

And what happens when you tell them you *don't* want something, especially if it's something they want you to want, do or have? When your parents insist that you do something that you don't want to do because you don't want it or you don't feel good doing it—like giving mean Aunt Jenny a kiss or playing with kids you don't like, "*Oh, you don't really mean that. Be nice, now, and go ahead and do it,*" you learn that the way you feel has little value in the adult world.

I call the bewilderment that results from this aspect of "socialization", the "Genesis of Confusion." Thus begins the process wherein you begin trusting what's been programmed into your mind over what's in your heart. After a while, you stop being conscious of what your heart wants, of what it's saying to you and you start focusing on all of the "*good reasons*" that reflect your parent's or society's values.

As time goes on, you get good at getting what you want by supplying the desired response to the question, "*Why?*" You learn from parental response what works and what doesn't. Sometimes it's a verbal response alone that does the trick and gets you what you want and sometimes it's the verbal response along with that cute way you smile when you ask for something. Either way, you learn that the currency expected from you and accepted by your caregivers almost always comes in the form of an explanation whenever you ask for something.

This "Why? - Because" ritual also teaches you to relate more to your head then your heart when you want something. Because you spend so much energy trying to figure out what your parents and the adults around you want to hear and see from you in order to have your wants granted, you begin to tailor your wants to what they deem acceptable. As you do this, the clear open channel to your heart, which is the origin of your creativity, your self-value and your desires, becomes narrower. After a while, the channel closes altogether and you forget how to connect with your heart, your creativity, your self-value and your desires. And with that, the saddest thing happens. You forget about a very important and essential birthright—you forget that you deserve to be happy.

And it *is* every person's birthright to be happy. When I work with clients, the most often expressed reason for their unhappiness and their failures is this: they don't feel they deserve to get or have what they want. Unfortunately, one of the unintended consequences of the socialization process is that most people have come to believe that they don't deserve to be happy.

The "Why – Because" indoctrination process costs you more and more every day, leading to the most detrimental loss of all, *the ability to trust your own feelings.* With your parent's emphasis on requiring an explanation from you when you want (or don't want) something, your little child mind begins to interpret this thusly—*"If there's this much questioning and drama when I express my feelings about wanting or not wanting something, then my feelings must be wrong and I can't trust them. It's best if I don't listen to my feelings or express them anymore. That way I won't feel bad or guilty for wanting anything."*

"People pleasers" and people who just can't make up their minds often get their start this way.

Ask yourself if you're still putting your most cherished hopes, dreams and wishes before the masses and by doing so, asking them in some form, if they approve of what you recognize as desirable and valid.

Too many of you can answer that question with a resounding, "Yes!" and that means you're a part of a vast majority of people who are still feeling unfulfilled, dissatisfied, disappointed and unhappy with the results of your life efforts. *Why?* Because the majority of your efforts to fulfill those cherished hopes, dreams and wishes are based on the approval of someone else and not based on your own sense of satisfaction and approval of yourself.

You're making the biggest mistake in the world if you want to achieve success and happiness—you're seeking someone else's approval and permission to be happy and that's a sure-fire method of insuring that you'll continue to live a life of personal, professional, emotional and spiritual unhappiness.

The most content people in the world are those who are the most satisfied with themselves. They're also the least likely to want or need approval from anyone, and that includes the world at large as well as those in their personal environments.

Content people have learned the number one element in achieving real success; they've learned to seek satisfaction—not approval—for themselves and therefore, their hopes, dreams and wishes. They've learned that the value they place on anything is directly based on the value they place on themselves and their belief in their right to happiness and fulfillment.

Yes, happiness, self-satisfaction, personal fulfillment and the pursuit of these precious and rewarding gifts—these are all rights that we're entitled to if we're willing to accept that truth and to work toward making our dreams come true.

I've lived and worked in several different countries and I've interacted with people from many diverse cultures. I've been shocked to discover that, in some areas of the world, what I consider a birthright—*getting what I want*—is looked upon as bad form! Once, in a London deli, I said to the counterman who was leaning over and scooping up the Greek salad I'd ordered, *"Please make sure you put extra feta cheese in my order."* He stood up as if he'd been hit by lightning, gave me a disapproving look, turned to his co-worker and said, *"Did you hear that!? She actually asked for what she wanted!"*

Without thinking, I immediately responded, *"Well, yes, how else am I going to get what I want?"*

I've thought about that incident a lot over the years. It told me a lot about the counterman and it told me a lot about myself. I still feel sad for that counterman. It was obvious to me that he was someone who didn't believe he or anyone else had the right to ask for what they wanted, even when it came to something as important as food. And it was just as obvious to me that I held and lived by the opposite tenet. I mean, what's the point of getting your favorite dish (or anything else) and not having it served the way you like?

One of my favorite quotes (which is the spiritual theme of my life and this book) is by the great designer, Karl Lagerfeld, *"This is the purpose of life—to get what you want. There are deeper things, but this is fun."* If you're happy, personally fulfilled and getting what you want, you won't have the inclination to be miserable and cause others in your world to be miserable, too. You'll want the world you live in to reflect that same kind of happiness, personal fulfillment and satisfaction. Your life won't be a breeding ground for fear, paranoia, jealousy or any of the other negative expressions that cause so many problems in our lives.

"Getting what you want? Being personally fulfilled? Seeking and enjoying satisfaction? But, isn't that selfish or hedonistic?" I've been asked those questions more times than I can remember. Somewhere along the way, we as a collective decided that being happy and feeling good about ourselves was self-indulgent and sinful. And once we came to that conclusion, we did everything we could to make sure that we felt guilty about pursuing and having every human beings natural birthright: a life of happiness, joy and satisfaction.

I thought a lot about those words—*selfish* and *hedonistic*—and I saw how, over time, their true meanings had become blurred and they'd come to be used as weapons by society as a whole and by ourselves as individuals to keep us tied to limiting, negative belief systems about our right to live in joy and happiness. Most of the time, when someone calls you selfish, it's because they want you to stop using your energy for yourself and start using it for them!

As I contemplated the use and impact of these potent words, *selfish* and *hedonistic*, I did what I always do whenever I want to better understand language and how we use it (or how it uses us)—I consulted the dictionary.

I like dictionaries, they make for very informative (and often interesting) reading. They're our collective's agreed upon arbiter when it comes to the meanings, sources and uses of the workhorses of our spoken and written communications—words. A good dictionary is thick and heavy and worth its weight in gold. This silent mediator acts as a bridge and holds a powerful place in our attempts to connect with and understand each other. Whenever we need to settle a dispute as to the meaning or origin of a word or phrase or we simply need clarity on a word or phrase's meaning, we've learned that we can consult this reference material and through doing so, come to an agreed upon understanding of what we're trying to get across to each other.

The word *"selfish"* is made up of two parts—the word *self* and the suffix, *ish*. Webster's dictionary defines the word, *"self,"* as *"a person or thing referred to with respect to complete individuality, as in, 'one's own self'."* The suffix, *"ish,"* is defined as *"having the characteristics of."* Therefore, in its simplest form, the word *"selfish"* literally means, *"of and for the self."*

In my experience, I've found that there are two kinds of selfishness—Positive or Spiritual Selfishness and Negative Selfishness. The distinction is an important one and it really ought to be noted in dictionaries.

Every living thing (and that includes us!) does whatever it is they do, positive or negative, in order to get something they want from doing it. Whether that something is money, attention, approval, pleasure, pain or power, that's what motivates us—it's the carrot at the end of the stick. When you do something for someone else, how does it make you feel? For most people, that feeling, good or bad, is your reward and it'll motivate you to repeat the act again and again.

We are "sensation junkies"—we react or respond to feelings. If we like the satisfaction we get from experiencing a sensation whether it's positive or negative, we'll keep doing whatever it takes to create and feel our own personal interpretation of satisfaction.

Positive or Spiritual Selfishness is joyfully and generously doing for or giving to yourself and/or someone else without heaping guilt upon yourself (or them). It's taking care of yourself. It's being good to yourself. It's living authentically, being guided by your heart, your connection to your Higher Power and your sense of self-value. It's giving yourself permission to live fully and enjoy the experience. It's not letting someone else's belief system (be it an individual's, a group's or society's) dictate what *"should"* be in your heart and mind and/or how you *"should"* live your life.

In our world, the words *"should"* and *"shouldn't"* get quite a workout. They're auxiliary verbs most often used to indicate duty, propriety or expediency. Overtime, they too, have become weapons wielded by society to "shake a finger" at someone in order to guilt them into feeling obligated to use their energy for the "finger shaker" instead of for themselves.

There is nothing bad or wrong with feeling good about yourself. There is nothing bad or wrong about wanting to be happy. As long as you handle what you want with integrity and responsibility and no one is harmed, you'll be fine.

Unfortunately, no matter how hard you try, sometimes things will go awry and you're going to make mistakes. However, and this is where integrity and responsibility come in, when you make a mistake—acknowledge it, apologize for it, forgive yourself and clean it up.

By the way, cleaning it up does not mean wallowing in emotion, giving your power to someone else or abandoning your dreams. If you handle the situation and yourself responsibly, guilt won't weigh you down and your mistake will become a powerful learning experience instead of unfinished business that crops up and blocks your path later on down the road. And lastly and very importantly, once you've handled the situation to the best of your ability—let it go and move on.

Life is an amazing experiential process. It offers us the opportunity to learn and grow from our experiences. And yes, some of those experiences can be gnarly, messy and downright embarrassing. If we heed the lessons these experiences offer us, though, we'll eventually become wise and successful.

Negative Selfishness is pretty much the way the word *"selfish"* is defined and described in most dictionaries, including Webster's—*"caring only for oneself and ones own interests, usually at the expense of and regardless of others."* That very clearly describes what we've all witnessed, experienced and been the foil of far too many times. Negative Selfishness is unhealthy narcissism and is at the heart of most of the problems in our world. We see it practiced by politicians, bureaucrats, corporations and criminals, as well as regular ordinary folks. Some of us even have family members who fit this description. Want proof of Negative Selfishness? Just read the news.

Negative Selfishness has nothing to do with joy or living authentically. And it's definitely not about being guided by your heart and being connected to your Higher Power. It's based on fear and lack and whenever it's practiced, somebody's going to get hurt.

Now—what about *"hedonism?"* That's a loaded word, isn't it? The word *hedonism*, comes from the Greek and is defined as *"the philosophy that pleasure or happiness is the highest good."* And that definition is correct. Taking joy and pleasure from being alive and being happy is indeed the highest good.

Again, in my experience, I've found that there are two kinds of hedonism—the positive kind, *Spiritual Hedonism*, and the morally bankrupt kind, *Toxic Hedonism*. Here too, I think the distinction ought to be noted in reference materials because it's a very significant distinction.

Unfortunately, all forms of the word, *hedonism*, have taken on a negative connotation in our society because so many people are taught from day one that suffering and the accompanying unhappiness and dissatisfaction with ourselves and our lives is actually a good thing. Why? Religious beliefs, cultural conditioning, fear, misery loving company, etc., etc., etc.—the list is long and everyone who spouts their reasons for choosing to live an unhappy and unfulfilled life has their own version of why it's OK to live like that.

Spiritual Hedonism, the art and practice of living with a heart and mind focused on joy and happiness, is our Divine right and sacred responsibility. When your heart is focused on joy and happiness, it's more creative, open and loving—you are closest to and in direct communication with the Divine and you don't have the need or desire to fill your life with anything but joy. You effortlessly become a magnet for your good and you automatically attract the very best to yourself.

When you're happy, you want others to be happy. You want the whole world to share and reflect the joy that you're feeling. You want that feeling of happiness, contentment and fulfillment to last forever because that's when you feel secure and safe and connected to all life. When your experience is this pleasurable, you feel endless, ageless and infinite and you feel and know that anything is possible. Being *hedonistic* is simply living in joy, acknowledging your value and coming from your heart and **that** is the highest and most profound form of spirituality that we can practice.

Children are the purist Spiritual Hedonists. Naturally innocent, they believe in the bounty of life. They listen to, live and operate from their hearts and that creates a wonderfully expansive space of joy and possibility. They believe anything can happen and they see life as a gift for them to expect, explore and receive the very best. When your heart speaks to you, the child of possibility within you is speaking. It is the job of You as the adult to listen with an open mind and heart and responsibly work with your inner child's heart's desire to make your dreams come true and thus attain the long sought after prize of a life lived in happiness, wholeness and contentment. Norman Podhoretz' quote expresses this truth beautifully, *"Creativity represents a miraculous coming together of the uninhibited energy of the child combined with the sense of order imposed on the disciplined adult intelligence."*

Toxic Hedonism is a negative expression and it's practiced by living with one's heart and mind focused on gluttony and waste. It springs from the fear of scarcity, of there not being enough of whatever it is you feel you need to have in order to survive—be it food, sex, power, money or any of a myriad variety of things.

Toxic Hedonism isn't about joy—it's poisonous and one of the more virulent forms of soul killing, mind numbing negative narcissism. It blinds you to the infinite, limitless possibilities that life offers. It makes you focus solely on your corporeal self, with no real thought or care for anyone or anything else, including your own heart, soul or well being.

"*Too much*" is an exhilarating state of mind, and as much as I love "*too much*," experience has taught me that too much of anything makes even the most natural and healthy substance or experience toxic. It's like the difference between using a little sugar to enhance the natural sweetness of something and dining exclusively on sugar. A little adds to the pleasure in life and doesn't harm your teeth or general health, while a steady diet of it will rot your teeth and cause you to suffer from malnutrition.

Isn't it time you chose for yourself what joy, satisfaction and success are?

Isn't it time you allowed yourself to enjoy and revel in your birthright of happiness, contentment and fulfillment?

To be content, to approve of yourself, to give yourself permission to accomplish what you want and then doing it—that always puts you in perfect alignment with the Divine. And when you're in perfect alignment with the Divine, you are a brilliant magnet, able to powerfully attract and manifest whatever you want and need.

So, are you ready to find out if you're really willing to have what you want? By answering the following two questions, you'll know exactly where you stand when it comes to supporting yourself and manifesting your vision.

1. **On a scale of 1 to 10 (10 being a lot and 1 being not at all): How much do you resonate with the Karl Lagerfeld quote, "*This is the purpose of life—to get what you want. There are deeper things, but this is fun.*"** _____

If your number is 1 through 5, you're entitled to think what you want, but that's where you're experiencing and processing your feelings—in your head. The more in touch you get with your heart and your feelings, the more able you'll be to tap into that fathomless source of natural, healthy entitlement that allows you to joyfully experience life and your participation in it as fun.

If your number is 6 or 7, you're spending a lot more time these days checking in with yourself and letting it be OK that sometimes, for no reason, you feel and revel in the joy of just being. Great—keep that up, because you're well on your way to allowing life to support you and your dreams.

If your number is 8 through 10—welcome aboard! Most, if not all of the time, no matter what's going on, you're not letting circumstances define you. You're more and more capable of living in the moment, listening with your senses and creating from the center of your being. And at that, being the point of the exercise, you'll find that you're living in the blissful splendor of perfect harmony with the rhythms of the Universe!

2. **On a scale of 1 to 10 (10 being the most and 1 being the least): How much of a commitment are you willing to make at this time in order to make your dreams come true?**

If your number is 1 through 5, you're not ready to commit to doing what it'll take to make your dreams a reality at this time. If you start out with such a low score, your internal strength and dedication aren't strong enough to sustain and support you when you encounter the inevitable "bumps in the road" that everyone encounters whenever they set out to make changes in their lives. The resulting disappointment will further undermine your confidence and make you even more hesitant to take a chance in the future on your dreams and yourself. Give yourself more time to examine your heart and contemplate your level of satisfaction with the way your life is turning out. Better to wait until your desire for wholeness and happiness exceeds your ability to settle for the status quo. While you're waiting, keep reading this book! You'll be showing the Universe that you're opening up to receive the limitless expansion that it wants you to have.

If your number is 6 or 7, you really do want your dreams to come true, but you're ambiguous about committing yourself to making it happen at this time. If you begin this quest on such unsure footing, you're likely to topple over if too many obstacles appear on your path or let the opinions of others sway you from doing what you must do in order to be successful. Spend more time building your commitment muscles by being with, talking to and reading about people who've accomplished their dreams. And keep reading this book—you'll find a lot of the commitment building exercises you need right here.

If your number is 8 through 10—congratulations—you've completed Step 1! You've given yourself permission to successfully live your birthright of happiness, fulfillment and contentment. 80-100% willingness will keep you going through all of the "seasons" of your grand adventure, through the abundant, fertile times as well as through the "dry spells" that are all a part of the process of achieving anything worthwhile. By giving yourself the invaluable gift of self-permission and combining it with what you'll learn in this book, you have everything you need to make your life what you want it to be.

By working with the exercises at the end of this chapter, you'll give yourself the opportunity to learn to reopen and/or expand the channel to your heart so that you can clearly express what you really want, first to yourself and then to others.

Work Book Exercises

"The first step to completing an overwhelming task is to complete the first step." —Anonymous

1. Listen to *Stage 1– Steps 1 through 3* of the Guided Imagery meditations that come with this book. Listening to this Guided Imagery meditation 15 minutes every day will help strengthen your determination and build your confidence as you begin the first step in the process of manifesting your vision. It will also help you connect your intuitive, creative, generating energy (feminine) to your intellectual, methodical, activating energy (masculine) which will heighten your level of magnetism and attract to you all manner of good luck, opportunities and helpful people and circumstances.

2. Before you go to bed, sit quietly for 15-20 minutes and listen to meditation music. Doing so will help you to more powerfully assimilate the experiences of your day and on an inner level, keep the center of creativity and desire—your heart chakra— open.

3. It's important to express gratitude. Expressing gratitude is more than just giving thanks. In addition to being an acknowledgement, it's also, to quote the author, Robert Emmons, *"a felt sense of wonder, thankfulness, and appreciation for life."* Gratitude places you in a state of grace and energetically positions you to be a magnet for the good you want to attract. Express gratitude to yourself for setting off on this journey to fulfillment. Express gratitude for your past and current circumstances that brought you to this point. Express gratitude for the people, events and luck that will come to assist you in achieving your goals. And if it's an appropriate reference for you, express gratitude to the Universe or your Higher Power for all of the inspiration that has been, is being and will be given to you.

4. Commitment Contract

I, _____,
wholeheartedly, 100% commit to manifesting my vision, (idea,
dream, project) of_____

_____
in its completed form by this date, _____.
I will take the necessary steps to begin, follow through and complete
my goal, regardless of any internal doubt or external pressure.

Signature_____
Date_____

Questionnaire

WHAT ARE SOME OF THE BELIEF SYSTEMS FROM YOUR FAMILY'S TREASURY OF "LIMITATION LITANIES?" LIST 3 OF THEM HERE:

1. _____
   _____
   _____
   _____
   _____

2. _____
   _____
   _____
   _____
   _____

3. _____
   _____
   _____
   _____

WHAT ARE SOME OF THE "BECAUSES" YOU USE NOW WHEN YOU'RE EXPLAINING WHY YOU WANT SOMETHING? LIST 3 OF THEM HERE:

1. _____
   _____
   _____
   _____
   _____

2. _____
   _____
   _____
   _____
   _____

3. _____
   _____
   _____
   _____
   _____

WHAT ARE SOME OF THE REASONS YOU CAN'T HAVE SOMETHING YOU WANT? (example: "With the economy the way it is today, I can't afford it.") LIST 3 OF THEM HERE:

1. _____
   _____
   _____
   _____
   _____

2. _____
   _____
   _____
   _____
   _____

3. _____
   _____
   _____

_____
_____

WHAT ARE SOME OF THE REASONS YOUR PARENTS GAVE YOU FOR NOT GRANTING YOUR WISHES? LIST 3 OF THEM HERE:

1. _____
_____
_____
_____
_____

2. _____
_____
_____
_____
_____
_____

3. _____
_____
_____
_____
_____

LIST THREE (3) LIMITING BELIEFS ABOUT YOURSELF:

1. _____
_____
_____
_____
_____

2. _____
_____
_____
_____
_____

3. _____
_____
_____
_____
_____

Chapter 2

The number "2" is a value determination number.
It relates to researching and determining the meaning and value of
something, be it a choice, an experience, an event, a relationship,
an idea, a product or a project. It's also a synergistic number; it uses
"co" energy—cooperate, communicate, connect, coordinate, cohesive,
combine, commit—anything that brings two or more people or
entities together in order to create something.

**This chapter will teach you how to determine the value and
viability of your idea. Here is where you take ownership of your
vision as you establish your foundation and begin to build
support for successfully bringing your goal into being.**

*"If you want to build a ship, don't drum up the people to gather
wood, divide the work, and give orders. Instead, teach them to
yearn of the vast and endless sea."*
—Antoine de Saint Exupery

Ninety desperate guys in three leaky boats. That's all it took
to change the world—ninety men whose options were so
limited or whose vision was so infinite (you decide) that
they elected to accompany Christopher Columbus on an adventure
that promised them great honors and untold wealth or a dismissive
footnote in history because they traveled too far in the wrong
direction and wound up sailing off the edge of the earth.

Often, whenever you decide to go after what you want, your
environment's view of you and your pursuit is the latter and your
view is the former. More often than that—YOUR view of yourself
and your pursuit is a strange combination of the two extremes.

If convincing Queen Isabella, who was going to stay ashore, to pay for the voyage was difficult, how did he convince ninety men who knew better, to sail with him? Unwavering commitment and passionate communication of his vision! That's really all he had as he invited others to join him and sign on to the most daring quest of their lives.

Yes—unwavering commitment, passionate communication and one more thing—courage. Christopher Columbus needed and had what we all need when we step outside the box that society has built for us—the courage to commit to manifesting his vision before he could do anything else to make his dream of global exploration and discovery a reality.

Once he'd found and aligned himself with his own personal courage, he had to find and nurture the courage it takes any time you want or need to communicate your vision to others, especially if you want to recruit them to help you achieve your goals.

And once you've found the personal courage to commit to the manifestation of your vision and the courage to communicate that vision to others, you then have to find the courage necessary to get on the "leaky boat," i.e., take the steps that are indispensable to the success of your visionary journey.

Do you know at what point most dreams fail? Here, at step 2. Why? There are two reasons, (1) now that you know what you want, you have to take practical steps—those mundane, but necessary, unglamorous things you have to do in order to create a solid structure and foundation for your dream and, (2) there is an energy that almost always shows up at this time—fear. It turns out that getting clear on what your goal is and your initial excitement about making your dream come true are generally followed by fear, doubt and worry.

Why is that?

Because you've just taken your dream from the very private and protected warm inner sanctum of your heart and introduced it to the conscious, cold light of your analytical and very much influenced by public opinion mind.

Since the mind habitually asks and answers its own questions about everything we decide to do, it often tries to convince us that we will suffer in some dramatic manner if we dare to do anything new or different.

Our minds are great at displaying what I call, *"flashcards of fear."* We've all had this experience. You get an idea to do something new or different and your mind eagerly searches for reasons that you should be afraid this new idea won't work, that you will fail. Your mind then retrieves every memory of failure and disappointment (yours and other people's) it can show you in order to discourage you from undertaking this new enterprise. Often, when these memories come to mind and are shown to you so quickly, they're like flashcards—a learning tool used to help you memorize a particular set of information, like math or a new language. It's important to keep in mind that these *"flashcards of fear"* can only show you scenes from the past—never the present or the future.

The *"flashcards of fear"* can be very effective at stopping you from taking the next important step at making your dream a reality. We all know people who talk about what they want to do and what they're going to do, but don't ever get around to doing enough or anything to bring their dream to fruition. These people always have an excuse for why they haven't made or can't make their dream come true. Rarely do they admit, to themselves or to anyone else, that at the very heart of their inertia is fear. Not the elaborate mental smokescreen that they've erected and are attempting to hide behind—just plain fear.

The fear in and of itself isn't the problem. In fact, fear is a natural, healthy, useful energy when we use it properly—to warn us of some impending danger. The real problem is what we allow this fear energy to do to us whenever we want to make changes in our lives. I've seen many people (myself included) put their dreams on hold or run away from their dreams because they've fallen into the trap that the *"flashcards of fear"* have set for them.

"Maybe they were right." "Who do I think I am?" "This is too hard." "What I want to do is impossible." These thoughts and others like them are the kinds of negative, debilitating, fearful thoughts that will often come up for you before you even tell another soul about your hope, your vision, your dream.

Whenever fear rears its head, please remember this mantra and repeat it—"*Fear is energy. Energy is innocent; it's what I do with it that determines the outcome.*"

Energy is a force that must be used. It doesn't care how it's used; it simply has to be used. When these fearful, negative thoughts, these *"flashcards of fear,"* begin to race through your mind, you have to quickly make a decision—to either use the energy of fear or to let the energy of fear use you. When fear rears its head, you must take the lead and steer this powerful force in the direction you want it to go. In other words, you must convert the energy of fear into the energy of courage.

How? First, consciously admit to yourself that at some point— OK, at many points—in pursuing and achieving your goal, you are going to be afraid. Then, when you do begin to feel fear, you must neutralize it by telling yourself the truth about what's going on in your physical world in that moment.

Let's practice this transformative technique right now. Imagine that you're feeling fear—"feel" the tension as it builds in your body. Now, look around you. Notice what's in front of, behind and to the right and left of you. Then ask yourself, "*Is anyone coming toward me in a threatening manner or with a weapon aimed at me?*" If the answer is no, ask yourself, "*Did I last eat what and when I chose?*" If the answer is yes, ask yourself, "*Do I sleep in a warm safe place of my choosing?*" If the answer is also yes—then you're probably in control of your circumstances and the fear energy you're experiencing is not acting as a warning signal; it's simply reacting to your vulnerable state of being as you contemplate change. As you do this technique, the fear and tension will leave your body and you'll return to a calm state. Sometimes, this technique only takes a few minutes to work and sometimes it takes longer. No matter how long it takes, stick with it and continue doing it until you feel your sense of power returning. As the knot in your stomach begins to melt, the paralysis in your muscles will be transformed into a powerful stimulant, vigorously impelling you toward your goal.

Next, get physical. Do something that requires you to be fully engaged physically, something that will occupy your mind and direct your energy in a constructive way. Go for a jog, paint the house, wash the car—it doesn't matter what you do as long as you're moving and giving that old fearful energy a new way of focusing and expressing itself.

Other great ways to neutralize fear energy are to do at least one of these simple, but powerful "truth" exercises:

1. Replace the false, negative chatter that's going on in your head with truthful, positive statements. When negative, non-supporting thoughts like, *"Why did I think I could do this—I don't know enough to ever succeed at achieving my goal,"* or, *"Who am I kidding, no one is going to want what I'm offering,"* enter your mind and start to undermine your confidence and rob you of your power, you take your power back by responding to each of those negative thoughts with a positive new thought. For example, when the negative thought, *"Why did I think I could do this—I don't know enough to ever succeed at achieving my goal,"* comes up, replace that negativity with the opposite thought—*"Every step I take and every person I interact with brings me more knowledge and experience as I move toward the successful attainment of my goal."* Or when the thought, *"Who am I kidding, no one is going to want what I'm offering,"* invades and violates your thought processes, replace it with, *"The history of civilization is proof that there is a receptive market for new ideas. Of course people are going to want what I'm offering."*

    Even if you don't believe what your replacement thoughts are telling you at first, your mind is still doing what it always does—logging these new thoughts in as truth. As you refute the negative thoughts with positive, opposite thoughts, you'll be simultaneously eliminating the space for negativity and creating a new, positive mindset that is based on processing the information you receive in a supportive, contributing manner to you.

2. You can neutralize fear energy and take your power back by writing out the questions from the technique we practiced previously and then writing your answers down so that you can see them in "black and white." As you write and read what you've written, you'll actually see that you really are in a safe space and your energetic field will change to one of calmness and trust in your surroundings.

3. This method is also very effective: write a list of your current fears on a piece of paper, and then tear that paper into little bits and throw them away. As simple as this sounds, it feels great and very empowering to rip those fears up and toss them out of your life.

All of these exercises will help you center and ground yourself, as well as, give you a "real time" experience of taking back your power. Notice how you feel as you do these exercises, especially the one we practiced. The tension begins to leave your body as soon as you answer the first question and by the time you've answered all of them, the most debilitating aspects of the tension are gone and you've found your light and your courage again.

Commit, Value, Communicate

Now that you clearly know what it is you want to create, do, make, or bring to fruition and you've learned how to deal with fear—what's next? How do you proceed? What is the most effective way to use your energy so that it produces the results you want?

You'll need to align yourself and your vision with your most powerful ally—the big "C"—Commitment. I can't stress enough just how important commitment is. Without it, you'd be forced to rely solely on luck and chance, which can only take you so far. By aligning your intention and desire with the principle and practice of commitment, you can't help but succeed in any endeavor.

Just what is commitment; what does that word mean?

Webster's dictionary defines commitment as a *pledge or a promise*—doing what you say you're going to do when you say you're going to do it. It involves dedication to achieving a goal. In a way, committing to achieve a goal is a lot like committing to a marriage. By making a commitment, you promise to use your energy for the successful outcome of the union (you and your goal) no matter what distractions might present themselves to you.

I'm sure you know by now that this isn't always an easy promise to keep. There are always distractions, our modern world is full of them. And you aren't always in the mood to honor your commitments. And...and...and... there are countless other reasons or excuses that'll present themselves to you when you *"just don't feel like it right now."*

When I *"just don't feel like it right now,"* i.e., keeping my commitment to my vision, I've trained myself to remember two of my favorite inspirational quotes:

"Commitment is what transforms a promise into reality. It is the words that speak boldly of your intentions. And the actions which speak louder than the words. It is making the time when there is none. Coming through time after time after time, year after year after year. Commitment is the stuff character is made of; the power to change the face of things. It is the daily triumph of integrity over skepticism" by Abraham Lincoln and William Hutchinson Murray's *"Until one is committed, there is hesitancy, the chance to draw back, always ineffectiveness. Concerning all acts of initiative (and creation) there is one elementary truth—the ignorance of which kills countless ideas and splendid plans—the moment one definitely commits oneself, then Providence moves too. All sorts of things occur to help one that would never otherwise have occurred. A whole system of events issues from the decision—raising in one's favor all manner of unforeseen incidents and meetings and material assistance—which no one could have ever dreamed would have come one's way. I have learned a deep respect for one of Goethe's couplets:*

'Whatever you can do, or dream you can—
begin it now.
Boldness has genius, power and magic in it.'"

In other words, the Universe will assist you, guide you, support you, even work miracles for you—but first you have to commit! And then you have to support your commitment by taking all of the appropriate actions that'll help you make your dream come true.

At the end of this chapter, in the work book section, you'll be able to create your own commitment statement that will clearly express your dream and your commitment to it.

Next, you must determine the value of your vision.

Value? What do you mean—value?

Again, let's refer to Webster's dictionary. There are many different variations on the definition of value. This is the one we'll use—value is defined as, *"worth determined by excellence based on desirability, usefulness or importance."*

Basically speaking, the value of anything is relative to what is important to you or what has meaning to you. Another way of putting this is—value means, *"what is it worth to me and what is it worth to others."*

OK—how do you measure worth and who determines the worth of something?

This step is explained in two parts and will help you answer two very important questions: 1- *What is my goal's value?* and, 2- *Who and what will help me achieve my goal?*

So—personal or professional—what is your goal's value to you, your environment, the world? Who is your market? What do they want or need in order to be so satisfied by your idea that they give their time, energy and/or money to it? And just as importantly, what do *you* want or need in order to be satisfied by achieving your goal? These are very important questions and you'll need to be able to answer these questions clearly if you're going to succeed.

Whether personal or professional, all goals follow the same paths to fulfillment, with a few differences separating them. Read both categories and feel free to learn from and use the information that best helps you succeed on your quest.

If your goal is a personal one:

What's a personal goal? On some level, every goal is a personal goal because you, your heart and mind are all involved. Here, a personal goal is defined as something that has meaning to you based on your own understanding of what is important to you. It's connected with what will make you feel satisfied with yourself and your accomplishments. Although it may involve others, it doesn't need the approval or appreciation of anyone but you. For example, suppose you want to learn the ancient Japanese art of origami or run a marathon or, as one of my clients wanted—to take control of her family's stock portfolio away from their financial consultant and manage her family's finances, herself. Those are examples of personal goals.

They're just as important as professional goals (sometimes, they're even more important) because you're paying attention to what your soul wants you do to and the reward for doing that is priceless.

By going within, you'll find the answers to the questions that will help you determine the value of your vision. Whether this is your first time undertaking self-examination on an inner level or you're an old hand at it, it's always an enlightening experience. There is a wealth of information within you; all you need to do is learn how to access and retrieve it so that you can make profitable use of it.

Going within is a process called by a variety of names—seeking insight, meditation, mindfulness, inner awareness—those are a few of the ways we describe this process. Guided imagery (sometimes called guided meditation), silent meditation, nature walks and gentle movement exercises like yoga and tai-chi are all inner level, going within techniques you can use to help access your inner awareness. You'll discover that the valuable insight you derive from devoting as little as 15 minutes at the beginning of your day to any of these methods is immeasurable.

To determine your vision's value to you, ask yourself:

- What does my goal mean to me—what is its true value to me?

- What does achieving my goal mean to me?

- Will achieving my goal enhance or change my life or me in some way; if so, how?

- How much do I believe in myself?

- What kind of assistance and support systems will I need in order to succeed?

- How committed am I to seeing this through?

- How willing am I to do what is required in order to make this happen?

- (If your personal goal involves other people) How will achieving my goal enhance or change my life and/or the lives of those who are close to me?

Being consciously aware of the answers to these questions opens a priceless, fathomless well of knowledge and continual inner support as you work to make your dream a reality.

In the work book section of this chapter, you'll be able to write out your answers to these very meaningful questions and you'll learn a lot more about yourself by completing this exercise.

Who will help you achieve your personal goal? In almost every case, no matter how personal your goal is, at some point you'll need the help of someone else. Often, others will be called in to assist you as you make your dreams a reality. Rarely can you do everything you need to do on your own.

Some of the "assistants" you'll meet and use in your quest are affirmations, role models, mentors, life coaches and support groups. Affirmations are important because they encapsulate in a few words, your vision, as well as inspire you as they remind you of your goal. For example, the affirmation that inspires and encourages me on a daily basis is also the inspiration for this book, *"This is the purpose of life–to get what you want. There are deeper things, but this is fun."* by Karl Lagerfeld.

Role models are great because they've done what you want to do—they've made their dreams come true. You can choose a role model who represents an energy, demonstrates a determination and/or achieves a victory you admire from any point in history. Their inspiring energy and spirit are infinite, and you can relate to and tap into them to bolster your energy and spirit. You'll find a list of possible role models in the appendix section at the back of this book.

A mentor is a person of wisdom that you can talk to in "real time" about your goal. They can give you advice and counsel you as to the most beneficial ways to move forward with your quest as well as uplift and inspire you when you need it. Sometimes a mentor has no expertise in the field of your quest. That's OK. As long as they understand you and the workings of the world and they're willing to share their life knowledge with you, they can be an invaluable ally for you.

A life coach serves a similar function as a mentor, with a few exceptions. They are paid trained professionals who work with you in a structured way in order to help you attain and sustain your vision. In addition to offering you structure, they also serve as an objective "mirror" for you during your process of successfully realizing your goal. One of the most valuable aspects of working with a life coach is that they hold a space for you to be accountable to yourself and your vision.

A support group, often led by a trained professional, is made up of individuals with related issues or objectives who meet on a regular basis to help themselves and one another by sharing experiences, knowledge, information and encouragement. Support groups are great at providing a sounding board for your ideas and concerns, as well as providing a feeling of camaraderie because all of the participants are on some sort of meaningful quest. Social networking sites are great places to find and connect with like-minded people, too. Some of the more popular ones are Facebook, Twitter or LinkedIn.

You'll find a list of suggested affirmations in the appendix section at the back of this book. You can use those affirmations or choose your affirmations from other sources. It really doesn't matter where you find your affirmations; what matters here is that they inspire and encourage you.

You'll find a list of possible role models in the appendix section at the back of this book, too. You can easily research them on-line. What you're looking for in a role model is someone you relate to and feel an affinity towards. It's best not to choose a popular celebrity or someone you're related to. We're drawn to a particular role model because they have a quality that matches and reflects something vital in us. It's not important to know what that something is, just that we relate to the person we're drawn to in some positive way.

You'll also find a list of possible mentors and social media sites in the appendix section at the back of the book. I can't overstate the importance of having a mentor or life coach whose viewpoint, wisdom and maturity you can count on. They take on the role of a guiding light in the fog and can offer the clear insight necessary to help you maintain and sustain balance and focus.

If your goal is a professional one:

A professional goal is one that advances you and your career in some way. It will enhance and/or expand your visibility in your chosen line of work. For example, landing an important new account, starting your own business, going back to school to learn new job skills or getting your MBA are all professional goals.

Much of the advice for achieving a professional goal is the same for someone with a personal goal, with a few exceptions. You'll benefit from affirmations, role models, mentors, life coaches and support groups, too.

The *"going within"* exercise will also work well for you. After all, you're the one who'll be making it happen and the more you know about yourself, the better.

In addition to the *"going within"* exercise, you'll also need to ask and answer these questions as a part of getting started in making your vision a reality.

- What is the value or profitability of this idea in dollar amounts or career achievement?

- What steps are required to achieve what I want?

- How much time will it take to complete my goal?

- How much money will it take to accomplish my goal?

- How committed am I to seeing this through?

- How willing am I to do what is required in order to make this happen?

- How much do I believe in my idea?

- How much do I believe in myself?

- What kind of assistance and support systems will I need in order to succeed?

- Will it help to belong to any organizations or associations?

In the work book section of this chapter, you'll be able to write out your answers to these questions so that you can begin to see in "black and white" how you'll need to strategize in order to achieve success.

Whether your goal is personal or professional, your greatest ally is research, research, research! I can't stress enough the importance of gathering information important to the success of your quest. Research isn't dull and doesn't have to be. Like a detective, you'll uncover a world full of sources and people who will be happy to help you if you just ask. There's the Internet, libraries, associations, professional groups and so much more just waiting to help you make your dreams come true. Each bit of information has the potential to lead you to a greater source of information. This is one of the most invigorating parts of the process of achievement—gathering knowledge.

The things you learn, the experiences you have, the people you interact with—none of these can be foretold before you set off on your quest. Each encounter is filled with limitless potential. True, some of the information you come across will be useless, but the information that is helpful and the experience of getting it—priceless!

Who do you need to talk to, communicate with and enlist aid from? This is the step where you choose allies. An ally is anyone who helps you, whether it's for five minutes or for the entire time you're working to achieve your goal. A long time ago I decided that the Universe and everyone in it wanted to help me get what I want. They don't necessarily know that yet, but as soon as I show up and let them know I'm on a quest, they realize that they want to be a part of my adventure and offer to help in whatever way they can.

I make it a habit to always ask whomever I'm speaking with about my quest if they can direct me to someone who can be of further assistance to me. People love this! Everyone knows someone or something that they wouldn't have thought of if you hadn't asked them that question. It lets them know that they are personally involved with making sure you're happy. And it lets them feel consciously connected to their own hopes, wishes and dreams, too.

On some level, they're adding their energy to your quest, which always serves to make them feel better and of course, it enhances your journey to success.

Long-term, as well as short-term allies for people with professional goals are often found in support groups called associations, clubs, alumni groups or chambers of commerce. Participating in these organizations is called networking. Social networking sites like Facebook, Twitter or LinkedIn are also excellent places to find allies and connect with like-minded people. These professional allies can do exactly what support groups for people with personal goals do—support you in your quest of manifesting your vision. Remember, the Universe and everyone in it really does want to help you get what you want. You just have to show up and let them know.

Work Book Exercises

"Commitment is doing the thing you said you'd do,
long after the mood you said it in is gone."
—Georg Zalucki

1. Listen to *Stage 1– Steps 1 through 3* of the Guided Imagery meditations that come with this book. Listening to this Guided Imagery meditation 15 minutes every day will help strengthen your determination and build your confidence as you continue the process of manifesting your vision. It will also help you connect your intuitive, creative, generating energy (feminine) to your intellectual, methodical, activating energy (masculine) which will heighten your level of magnetism and attract to you all manner of good luck, opportunities and helpful people and circumstances.

2. Before you go to bed, sit quietly for 15-20 minutes and listen to meditation music. Doing so will help you to more powerfully assimilate the experiences of your day and on an inner level, keep the center of creativity and desire—your heart chakra—open.

3. It's important to express gratitude. Expressing gratitude is more than just giving thanks. In addition to being an acknowledgement, it's also, to quote the author, Robert Emmons, *"a felt sense of wonder, thankfulness, and appreciation for life."* Gratitude places you in a state of grace and energetically positions you to be a magnet for the good you want to attract. Express gratitude to yourself for setting off on this journey to fulfillment. Express gratitude for your past and current circumstances that brought you to this point. Express gratitude for the people, events and luck that will come to assist you in achieving your goals. And if it's an appropriate reference for you, express gratitude to the Universe or your Higher Power for all of the inspiration that has been, is being and will be given to you.

<u>PERSONAL GOAL QUESTIONAIRE</u>

Remember, the more consciously aware you are of the answers to these questions, the more you'll be able to connect with your powerful reservoir of knowledge and strength as you work to make your dream a reality.

1. What does my goal mean to me—what is its true value to me?

_____
_____
_____
_____
_____
_____
_____

2. What does achieving my goal mean to me?

_____
_____
_____
_____
_____
_____
_____

3. Will achieving my goal enhance or change my life or me in some way; if so, how?

_____
_____
_____
_____
_____
_____
_____

4. How much do I believe in myself?

_____
_____
_____
_____
_____
_____
_____

5. How committed am I to seeing this through?

_____
_____
_____
_____
_____
_____
_____

6. How willing am I to do what is required in order to make this happen?

_____
_____
_____
_____
_____
_____
_____

7. Who will help me achieve my personal goal?

_____
_____
_____
_____
_____

----

8. What kind of support systems will I need in order to succeed?

----

9. If my personal goal involves other people—how will achieving my goal enhance and/or change the lives of those who are close to me?

PROFESSIONAL GOAL QUESTIONAIRE

The more clearly you answer these questions, the easier it'll be for you to make your vision a concrete reality.

1. What is the value or profitability of this idea in dollar amounts or career achievement?

_____
_____
_____
_____
_____

2. How much time will it take to complete my goal?

_____
_____
_____
_____
_____

3. How much money will it take to accomplish my goal?

_____
_____
_____
_____
_____

4. On a scale of 1 to 10—10 *being highest*—how committed am I to seeing this through?

_____
_____
_____

----

5. On a scale of 1 to 10—*10 being highest*—how willing am I to do what is required in order to make this happen?

----

6. How much do I believe in my idea?

----

7. How much do I believe in myself?

----

8. What kind of assistance and support systems will I need in order to succeed?

9- Will it help to belong to any organizations, associations or social networking sites?

_____

_____

_____

_____

_____

10- If the answer to question 9 is "Yes," which organizations, associations or social networking sites will I join?

_____

_____

_____

_____

_____

Your Commitment Statement

"Unless it is supported by a practical plan, no mundane, creative or spiritual concept can come to successful fruition."

—Sheilaa Hite

You're never more than two hours away from actually manifesting your dream! That's the average length of time it takes to write your commitment statement. When you've finished writing it, you'll have produced the first physical manifestation of your vision! It's a descriptive plan that states clearly what is needed to physically manifest and complete the whole project. The statement must be clear, direct and specific. It will act as a compass for you as you enact the steps that'll guide you to making your vision a concrete reality.

Your commitment statement will also become an attracting force, a magnet that will do exactly what this excerpt from William Hutchinson Murray's inspiring quote promises— *"the moment one definitely commits oneself, then Providence moves too. All sorts of things occur to help one that would never otherwise have occurred. A whole system of events issues from the decision—raising in one's favor all manner of unforeseen incidents and meetings and material assistance—which no one could have ever dreamed would have come one's way."*

Follow the example of the sample commitment statement below and in a separate notebook, write out your Commitment statement and work with it until your goal is clearly stated and can be clearly understood by you and anyone you read it to.

Once your Commitment Statement is clear, direct and specific, write it out on the lined page that follows the sample commitment statement. Once you've done that, you'll be ready for the next step— clearly communicating your vision and gathering allies to help you in your endeavor.

Sample Commitment Statement

MY COMMITMENT on SEPTEMBER 12, 1995: I will write out in full, six scripts for my guided meditation series—one for each guided meditation, along with the one introduction I will use for all six of my guided meditations. I will research and clearly know what I must do to successfully and profitably, produce, market and sell my CD's to the public, including gathering the information I need by speaking with audio recording distributors about U.S. and international marketing for my guided meditation series. I will find and secure the rights to the music and cover artwork I want to accompany each meditation. I will research the cost of this project and find/create the best price and technicians to produce, market and sell my guided meditation CD series. I will gather all of this information into a presentation package so that I can approach and meet with prospective investors who will provide the funding to produce my series of six guided meditation CD's. I will complete all of this by October 24, 1995.

My Commitment Statement

MY COMMITMENT on (month)_____, (date)_____, (year) ____

_____
_____
_____
_____
_____
_____
_____
_____
_____
_____
_____
_____
_____
_____
_____
_____
_____
_____
_____
_____
_____
_____
_____
_____
_____
_____

Chapter 3

The number "3" is a review and decision number.
It represents the first or initial stage of completion of any endeavor.
It's the number that relates to using all of your senses in the
gathering and processing of information and ideas, and to
communicating them to others and/or yourself in a new way. The
number of discernment and sorting, it's the point at which you can
look at your original idea and see what it's shaping up to be so that
you can determine what it needs in order to move forward to the
successful completion of your goal.

**You have now reached the first stage of completion
of your project. This chapter will teach you how to communicate
the value and viability of your idea to yourself and others. Here is
where you begin to seek and gather support as you invite others to
participate in your quest.**

*"Whether you think you can or
think you can't, you're right."*
—Henry Ford

Can You Make A Decision?
The Southern Belle Syndrome

Recently, I was in New Orleans, Louisiana indulging in one
of my favorite pastimes—attending a trade show in support
of a friend. I love traveling and interacting with people from
all walks of life and I'm always curious about the inner workings of
just about everything. I also love supporting my friends, so helping a
friend out at one of these professional gatherings is like a mini-
vacation to me.

As her assistant, my only duty the first day was to make sure the supplies my friend had shipped ahead to the hotel, got to her booth at the convention center before the start of business on opening day of the show. We were pre-registered and all I had to do was stop by the registration desk at the convention center and pick up my name tag so that I could be admitted into the exhibitor's hall. *"No problem,"* I thought. We'd gone to the convention center the day before to set up her booth and had been given instructions and shown the lay-out as part of the participant's orientation.

We felt confident that all would flow smoothly as she went to a pre-show meeting at the convention center ahead of me. As I accompanied the hotel porter who was carting my friend's supplies on the short walk from the hotel to the convention center, I felt wonderful—it was a beautiful day and the porter's Katrina survivor story, though sad in parts, had a triumphant outcome. *"Great,"* I thought, *"nothing could possibly mar the way I feel now."* Once I reached the registration counter, however, I quickly realized that *"nothing"* is in the eye of the beholder as well as being an amorphous concept that can only hold its form if it's supported by its current environment and/or circumstances.

There were at least six women behind the counter at the registration desk, ranging in age from about forty to the late fifties. Except for the one who was helping me, they were all idle. I gave the clerk my name and the name of my friend's company and told her that I was pre-registered and that I wanted to pick up my name tag so that I could enter the exhibit hall.

As I waited for her to find my name and print out my I.D. tag, I tried phoning my friend to let her know I'd arrived at the convention center and the porter and I would be delivering her supplies to her at her booth in a couple of minutes. My cell phone couldn't get a signal inside the convention center, but I reasoned that it wasn't such a big deal because I'd have her supplies to her in time for her to set up her booth before the hall opened to the show's attendees.

After about five minutes of computer searching and with an increasingly befuddled look on her face, the clerk told me that my name and the company name were listed but I couldn't have a name tag because they'd given my name tag to my friend. She went on to explain that neither I, nor the porter, could gain entry to the exhibit hall without the name tag and that nothing could be done about it.

By the look on her face and the slightly unfocused look in her eyes, I could see that I was facing someone who had obviously "failed upward" so I decided to just focus on getting my friend's supplies to her and I'd work on getting my name tag later. I explained the situation and asked if 1: either one of the registration clerks could go in with me while the porter and I dropped the supplies off or 2: one of them could go in without me but with the porter and deliver the supplies herself or 3: one of them could go in without the porter or me and tell my friend that I was having difficulty getting in and ask her to come out and get her supplies or 4: one of them could come up with something that would work well for all of us.

My initial decision to speak slowly and softly with this group was validated, because just the fact that I was standing there insisting that there must be some solution to the problem and then providing them with a set of possible solutions was causing them very obvious distress.

With each suggestion, the befuddlement, fear, anxiety and out-right confusion on their faces increased exponentially. I swear—their eyes were practically rolling to the backs of their heads! At this point, understanding that being able to logically consider my requests was far more than they had been prepared for, I asked to speak to someone in a position of authority.

My request seemed to alleviate the confusion somewhat as they all set to looking around for who that might be. One of them disappeared into a back area and reappeared with a very pleasant looking woman of about thirty. She approached me, introduced herself as a supervisor and asked if she could be of assistance. After witnessing the events (or rather, non-events) that had preceded her arrival, the response that came unbidden from me was, "*Can you make a decision?*" She was taken aback and asked, "*What do you mean?*" I replied, "*Can you make a decision? No one here can answer a simple question or make a decision. I need someone who can make a decision. Are you that person?*"

I knew then, that I'd gone too far, because she'd begun to swoon and her eyes were losing focus. I watched, fascinated, as she tried to regain her bearings. Finally, she steadied herself and touching her supervisor pin, she asked, *"What do you want?"*

I responded, *"I need to know if you can make a decision, because I don't want to spend another ten minutes explaining the situation and coming up with solutions that nobody here is capable of acting on."* "Oh," she said, *"I don't know if I can make a decision but what is the problem and what are the solutions you came up with?"*

Deciding that this was a huge improvement over everything else that had transpired and realizing that this was probably the best that it was ever going to get, I took a chance and briefly explained my situation, the problem and the four solutions I had come up with.

To her credit, she did try to work with what I'd just given her. I know because I saw the wheels turning. Finally, she seemed satisfied with what she'd grasped and as she smiled at me, she confidently responded, *"I understand now. You're saying that you want me to escort the hotel porter into the hall and have him deliver the supplies while you wait out here for your friend to come and get you—right?"*

I had to admit that it was a pretty creative interpretation of what I'd said. So much so, that I realized/decided that some huge other worldly phenomenon was taking place and I was being shown the inner workings of an alternate reality. Whenever that happens, I've learned to just go with it. *"No, that isn't what I said, but if that will get the supplies into the hall and to my friend's booth—fine."*

Just then, my friend came out of the exhibition hall. It turned out that my experience with the registration clerks was simply a continuation of hers. When she'd tried to get her name tag, she was told that although her company name was listed, they couldn't find her name and even though she showed them her driver's license and her business card as proof that she was who she was claiming to be, she couldn't get a name tag and gain entry to the hall.

Frustrated and fighting incredulity, she pointed to her watch and stated, *"You're about to make me late. I'm from New England and we don't like to be late, so you'd better do something."* That's when, panicked at such a show of directness, clarity and strength, they found my name on the list and gave her my name tag so that she could attend her meeting.

The supervisor, erroneously thinking she was getting off easier by dealing with my friend, offered to personally take the supplies into the hall and escort my friend to her booth.

With that finally taken care of, I'd completed my 'assistant' obligations for the day. I told my friend that I was going to spend the rest of the day exploring New Orleans and I'd be back at 4:30 that afternoon to help her close down her booth. As we said our good-byes, the supervisor assured us that she'd get everything straightened out and I'd have no trouble getting my I.D. tag when I returned.

After a great and magical day exploring the Crescent City, I went back to the convention center at 4:30 that afternoon. There was a different clerk at the registration counter. She looked at me, smiled very sweetly and greeted me with, *"Oh, I remember you. You were here earlier today."* Another clerk, less diplomatically stated, *"Yes, you were here this morning."*

I had to suppress a big laugh as I thought, *"Hmm, I guess I made a memorable impression."*

After an awkward pause, the clerk who'd greeted me upon my return offered to help me by getting my name tag. I couldn't help smiling as I imagined the meeting they must have had about their interaction with me after I'd left that morning. Although she was very polite, I think this woman must have drawn the short straw at the meeting.

She directed me to a computer terminal at the far end of the counter, away from the other clerks. *"Hmm,"* I thought, *"is she afraid that I'll implode or explode?"* I gave her my name and the company name and in no time, they both came up—progress! However, there was a glitch. She explained that my friend was sharing a booth with another vendor, and no booth could have more than two people in it!

What!? That was absolutely ridiculous. In all the years I'd worked at trade shows, I'd never heard that one! It was beyond being merely non-sensical—it was ludicrous in ways that defied description. So ludicrous, in fact, that I didn't even bother to get upset. I just looked at her and calmly asked to speak with someone in authority. She insisted that that wouldn't do any good because rules were rules and that one couldn't be broken.

Again, I calmly asked to speak with someone in authority. Finally, with a sigh, she called for someone and a man approached, announced that he was the supervisor and asked if he could help. I noticed that all of the clerks at the counter worshipfully focused their attention on him.

I gave him as brief and concise an account as I could about my frustrating interactions with the registration process, rules and clerks. He listened attentively and very casually asked, "Oh, so you just want to be able to get into the hall?" I told him that that was what I'd been wanting all along. He nonchalantly turned to the clerk and said, "Give her a name tag."

The clerk's demeanor changed as she looked at him and repeated his simple directive, "Give her a name tag." Her face brightened, her posture straightened, her energy became clearer and the expression on her face told me she had just experienced something akin to the second coming.

She was still too flustered by his presence to actually carry out his directive, so he leaned over and tapped two keys on the keyboard. She exclaimed, "Ohh!" as the printer began printing out my name tag. I was relieved and happy, though, that she proved capable of being able to put the name tag into a holder and give it to me with a comparatively minimal amount of difficulty.

The entire registration desk episode was like something from "The Twilight Zone." It was such an eerie, icky feeling that, at times, I actually started to look around for the TV cameras—"This can't be real. It has got to be some sort of prank!" Sadly, there were no cameras and it wasn't a prank. It was real and it was painfully obvious that the women working there had no sense of themselves, their value, their power or how to direct that power effectively. This really was how they did their jobs and, I suspected, lived their lives.

I've been in third world countries where women had little to no real human rights and they demonstrated a higher sense of self worth than those clerks. The clerks and the first supervisor were completely helpless to think for themselves or make any kind of clear decision until a man came along who could make a decision and take action for them.

When I shared this sad, perplexing experience with my friends, my northern women friends were as mystified as I was by the whole experience. However, my southern women friends smiled ruefully and all said the same thing, *"You had a Southern Belle experience. Although it's not as pervasive as it used to be, there are still a lot of women in the South who are raised with the belief that the only value they have is reflected in their ability to get a husband, no matter what the cost and the only way to do that is to display their desirability by being completely helpless and depending on a man to do their thinking for them. It's very threatening to these women to make a decision about anything that might reveal to themselves or the world that they can actually think for themselves."* (It should be obvious by now that neither my friends—regardless of where they come from—nor I, are "Southern Belle" types. We're far too clear, confident and direct for that.)

Every moment in life is a teaching moment. Every experience we have, has the potential to demonstrate something that can bring real and lasting value to us. This *"Southern Belle"* experience very clearly demonstrates the importance of consciously using <u>both</u> your generating, receptive, feminine energy <u>and</u> your activating, manifesting, masculine energy in a balanced manner if you're going to be successful at accomplishing anything meaningful in your life.

Energy is the power force that runs our lives and each one of has access to and must balance the two very distinct forms of it—feminine energy and masculine energy. These designations don't relate to gender, but rather to modes of expression. Feminine energy is life's power generator; the part of us that yearns, senses and nurtures. It's an amorphous, receptive, intuitive, bonding energy. Masculine energy activates and directs the force of feminine generating power and channels it to provide us with our needs and desires. It's a conscious, logical, action oriented energy.

In short—feminine energy magnetizes, feels and desires and masculine energy is magnetized and thinks and gets. That's the way creation works in nature. When these two energies of intuition and logic are balanced; we're in harmony with the flow of life and things work well for us. When they're out of balance, there can be no real harmony in any part of our lives and we are left to deal with the resulting discord.

Because of their emulation of what they perceived as a feminine ideal—helplessness—those women at the registration desk had a very highly developed relationship with their feminine energy and a very poor relationship with what their culture had taught them to perceive as dangerous—their masculine energy. They're good at needing and yearning and very much out of touch with thinking and getting when they're out in the world on their own. Sadly, because of this, they're very much out of balance. (In all probability, they've attracted mates who are just as imbalanced with their feminine energy as these women are with their masculine energy.)

Step three is the First Stage of Completion in any enterprise. Here is where you'll put your idea before a select group of people who can help you manifest your goal. In order to do this successfully, you'll have to be in conscious balanced communication with both your feminine—your intuitive, nurturing energy and your masculine—your focused thinking and getting energy. As you combine both aspects of your energy, pay attention to what you're thinking and feeling as you sort through the information that you've gathered and will continue to gather. (This is useful advice regardless of what you're working on.)

Feelings aren't bad or negative. After all, strong feelings—love, hate, joy, anger, desire—are all fueled by an even more powerful emotion—passion. And being passionate about your idea or vision is what you'll need to be if you're going to successfully bring it to fruition. Fear can also be a strong emotion. If it's warning you about impending danger—that's a good thing. If it's an irrational fear and you make your choices based on that type of fear, you'll undermine yourself and the successful outcome of your quest.

If you're feeling emotional or uncomfortable about something you're trying to decide on—set it aside and come back to it later when you can examine it more objectively, because the wrong kind of emotion will impair your decision making process.

The choices and decisions you make about your process and the progress of your vision at this point are very important because you're creating the "map" that'll get you to your goal. Here, you must logically and intuitively step into the realm of unembellished specificity and take your vision apart—"break it down" into individual parts—so that you can begin to see what type of organization it'll take to bring it to fruition. Admittedly, this isn't always easy to do when you're talking about your dreams, but it is very necessary.

How do you do this?

First, you need to look at your original idea, your vision, by reading your commitment statement. As you do so, you'll notice that each sentence in your commitment statement works as a directive, giving you information and pointing you in the direction of where you need to focus your energy so that you can identify and make clear what steps you need to take in order to successfully complete your goal.

Next, you'll need to look at all of the pertinent information you've gathered on your own—via outside sources and your intuitive feelings—as well as from researching the appropriate mentors, life coaches, associations and organizations recommended in the Appendix at the back of the book.

And third, you'll need to combine all of the information that relates to your quest, so that you can organize it and itemize it for your instruction guide—your "map".

Follow the example of the sample form below and in a separate notebook, write out your "Steps Necessary to Complete My Goal," and work with it until you have a clear, step-by-step set of instructions that will serve as an easy to understand guide, reminder and accountability tool for successfully getting you to your goal. It's also a measuring tool so that you can see where you are as you pursue the realization of your quest.

Once your "Steps Necessary to Complete My Goal" instruction guide is clear, direct and specific, write it out on the lined pages that follow the sample instruction guide. Once you've done that, you'll be ready for the next step: taking the actions that'll complete the foundation and begin the structure for manifesting your vision in material form.

Another advantage of being so thorough as you create this assignment is that you get to consciously see and experience what it actually takes to make something meaningful happen. You'll have an opportunity to stop taking yourself for granted as you acknowledge yourself with each move you make on the way to creating your success.

This exercise will take some time because, like a recipe, it's very detail oriented. It's worth it, though. If you try to avoid being specific as you do this exercise, you'll end up leaving out some key points and, as with a recipe, you'll be disappointed with the "dish" you create.

And remember, this itemized, instructional guide you're creating isn't written in stone. In life, as you progress, some things are bound to change. It's the same with your journey of manifestation. Don't be afraid to make the necessary adjustments to keep you moving forward toward your victory. Make sure to leave enough room after each item on the list so that you can make notes about your experiences and interactions with each step.

Work Book Exercises

"Half of our mistakes in life stem from feeling where we ought to think, and thinking where we ought to feel."
—John Churton Collins

1. Listen to *Stage 1– Steps 1 through 3* of the Guided Imagery meditations that come with this book. Listening to this Guided Imagery meditation 15 minutes every day will help strengthen your determination and build your confidence as you continue the process of manifesting your vision. It will also help you connect your intuitive, creative, generating energy (feminine) to your intellectual, methodical, activating energy (masculine) which will heighten your level of magnetism and attract to you all manner of good luck, opportunities and helpful people and circumstances.

2. Before you go to bed, sit quietly for 15-20 minutes and listen to meditation music. Doing so will help you to more powerfully assimilate the experiences of your day and on an inner level, keep the center of creativity and desire—your heart chakra— open.

3. It is important to express gratitude. Expressing gratitude is more than just giving thanks. In addition to being an acknowledgement, it's also, to quote the author, Robert Emmons, *"a felt sense of wonder, thankfulness, and appreciation for life."* Gratitude places you in a state of grace and energetically positions you to be a magnet for the good you want to attract. Express gratitude to yourself for getting to this first stage of completion of your project. Express gratitude for the people, experiences, and blessings that have assisted you in getting to this point. And if it's an appropriate reference for you, express gratitude to the Universe or your Higher Power for all of the inspiration and courage that have been, is being and will be given to you.

Sample STEPS NECESSARY TO COMPLETE MY GOAL
Instruction Guide

STEPS NECESSARY TO COMPLETE MY GOAL:
September 12 – October 24, 1995

1. Write out each guided meditation and the introduction.

    a. Sit at computer 2 hours a day, 3 days a week—Monday, Tuesday and Thursday from 10:00am to 12:00p—and write the meditations and the introduction.

2. Speak with Sarah re: her knowledge and information on audio recordings and distributors.

    a. This is the 1st order of business at our meeting tomorrow.

3. Speak with Scott re: his knowledge of audio recordings, the market for them, audio distribution and distribution companies.

    a. Meet with him on Friday, Sept. 22, 1995.

    b. Make a list of the distributors he recommends.

4. Visit book and CD stores in order to see what's being sold and how it's being sold.

    a. Call 1st and find out if and what they carry in audio series.

    b. Visit stores until I'm clear about how I want to package and present my guided meditation series.

5. Speak with and/or meet with audio distributors re: my CD's.

    a. Call and question each distributor re: requirements, percentages, territories and payment.

    b. Speak with different distributors everyday until I have the information I need.

6. Speak with and/or meet with musicians, publishing companies and BMI executives.

   a. Talk with Edward re: meeting with Brenda at BMI.

   b. Talk with Edward re: music and musicians for my guided meditation series.

   c. Talk with Scott re: music from existing music CD's and getting permission to use it.

   d. Go to Malibu Shaman, listen to music CD's and choose the music I want to use.

   e. Get publishing company information from existing audio and CD inserts and contact the publishers.

7. Speak with and/or meet with all of the technicians necessary to manifest my CD's—producers, recording engineers, as well as owners of recording studios, duplicators, packagers, printers, artists for cover art.

   a. By Wednesday, Sept. 27, 1995, make list of all technicians needed to complete CD's.

   b. Contact and meet with each of them by Oct. 3, 1995 and get their price lists for their services.

8. Report to class each week on my progress as well as enlist their assistance in any problem solving.

   a. Keep a journal of my activities, my results and my feelings.

   b. Talk with my "support-partner" the agreed upon 3 times a week re: support.

9. **Visualize**: 5 minutes before I begin each day's work on this project and before I go to sleep each night, I'll visualize my presentation package for my CD's being received, listened to, read, loved, wanted and invested in by all of the investors I

present it to in order to have my guided meditations recorded, packaged and promoted profitably for all involved.

Steps Necessary to Complete My Goal

_____
_____
_____
_____
_____
_____
_____
_____
_____
_____
_____
_____
_____
_____
_____
_____
_____
_____
_____
_____
_____
_____
_____
_____
_____
_____
_____
_____
_____
_____

Chapter 4

The number "4" is a foundation number.
It relates to the foundation, core and support of your endeavor and
denotes the beginning of the physical part of the manifestation
process as you objectively move from the planning stage to the
building and doing stage.

**This is usually the stage where one loses passion or enthusiasm
because this is where the work to achieve your goal becomes
mundane. At this stage, you must begin building and make sure
the foundation you need for the success of your endeavor is solid
and strong.**

*"If you have built castles in the air, your work need not be lost;
that is where they should be. Now put foundations under them."*
—Henry David Thoreau

You've just finished creating your own very detailed "Steps
Necessary to Complete My Goal" instruction guide. After
completing such an intense exercise, you might be
wondering, *"Is this much detail really that important?" "Is it necessary to
go through all of this in order to accomplish anything?" "Just how effective is
this painstaking, time-consuming part of the process, anyway?"*

Yes, this very detail oriented step <u>is</u> necessary, effective and
important. It leads you to the information that will help you build
the foundation for the success of your vision. Just as with building a
house, the foundation is one of the most important parts of the
entire process. The foundation supports and holds the weight of
the structure. If a building is built with an amazing design and state-

of-the-art materials and tools but has a shallow or faulty foundation, the building won't be able to stand very long and will eventually collapse. The same holds true for building anything else. The building of the foundation is the most important part because it'll support and hold the weight of the success of your vision.

(Sometimes the foundation takes longer to build than the actual structure of a building. In some California beach cities, for instance, in order to build an ocean front home, the builder must get many permits, go through lots of inspections and spend up to two years constructing the proper sanctioned foundation *before* they can even think about building the rest of the house!)

The Commitment Statement and "Steps Necessary to Complete My Goal" instruction guide work hand-in-hand. In addition to being your "aide memoire" and progress gauge, they are also a "shopping list" of sources, tasks and contacts you'll need in order to manifest your firm, supportive, foundation and vision. Your Commitment Statement will help you to remember and focus your energy and attention on what your goal actually is. Your "Steps Necessary to Complete My Goal" instruction guide will help you move forward in an organized, step-by-step manner, reminding you of what you've done, are doing and still need to do, as well as with whom.

The sample Commitment Statement in Chapter 2 and "Steps Necessary to Complete My Goal" instruction guide in Chapter 3 are mine—they're the first ones I wrote when I initially created and began to teach this system.

When I began my project, my vision was a very simple one. So simple, in fact, that I had no idea how transformational it was and how far it would take me.

What I wanted was an appealing proposal package—sheets of paper with tantalizing information on them in an attractive presentation folder.

What I intended to do with that proposal package was entice prospective investors to advance the money I needed in order to record, produce, package, successfully market, distribute and profitably sell my guided meditation series.

What happened as a result of completing Steps 1, 2 and 3 was more than I could have imagined. It was the living embodiment of Joseph Campbell's great quote, *"Follow your bliss. If you do follow your bliss, you put yourself on a kind of track that has been there all the while waiting for you, and the life you ought to be living is the one you are living. When you can see that, you begin to meet people who are in the field of your bliss, and they open the doors to you. I say, follow your bliss and don't be afraid, and doors will open where you didn't know they were going to be. If you follow your bliss, doors will open for you that wouldn't have opened for anyone else."*

So, just what did happen with my project? Everything went according to the plan laid out in the "Steps Necessary to Complete My Goal" instruction guide until I acted on the advice I got from Sarah in Step 2. She suggested that I contact a mutual acquaintance who was a composer. Sarah felt that she would be a wealth of information about the audio recording process. I made an appointment to meet with the composer the following week and I continued with the rest of the steps.

As I sorted through and followed up on the advice I received from the people on my list as well as the people they referred me to, I began to trust myself and my vision more and I began to feel that I would be successful in completing it. The word I'd use to describe the way I'd begun to feel is "empowered." Webster's defines empowered as, *"to be enabled or endowed with; to be given the confidence to do something."*

I could see that I'd be able to get the information I needed to put the investor's information package together and that encouraged me even more. I began to visualize myself in meetings with potential investors and wowing them so much with my thorough and beautifully presented proposal that they were begging me to let them invest their time, money and expertise in my project. I was so certain that I'd get the backing I needed, I could actually see myself in a recording studio, recording my guided meditations within the next three or four months.

During the second week of following through on my commitment, I met with the composer. I learned that she was also a recording engineer and audio producer with her own recording studio. She gave me a tour of her studio and offered me a package deal. In addition to providing the music for my guided imagery meditations, she'd sign the music rights over to me as well as produce and record my meditations for an affordable price! She also knew of a reputable duplicator and packager I could use.

Wow! I started out with the intention of just gathering information; pieces of paper with facts and figures on them, so that I could solicit help from investors in getting my meditation CD's recorded! Now, just a few days into starting my project, I had to consider the possibility of going way beyond mere pieces of paper and actually recording and packaging the meditations in an excellent studio at a cost I could afford!

I had a very good plan, but now, my vision seemed to be taking on a life of its own. How was this happening? Where did all of this come from!?

I attribute this wondrous occurrence to something I call, *"The Alignment."* "The Alignment" is energetic mirroring. When you align your intention, your heart, your energy and your focus with your goal, the Universe will always align itself with you and your vision. This energetically empowered 'partnership' works as a magnet to attract you to the Universe's assistance and to attract the Universe's assistance to you. This is often referred to as "luck." Webster's defines luck as, *"the force that operates, for good or ill, in a person's life to shape events or opportunities."* Luck comes from being the energetic embodiment or mirror of what you want to manifest in the world. The Universe aligns itself with you and reflects or mirrors that energetic embodiment which results in the physical manifestation of what you think, desire and envision.

"Good luck" comes from being and staying in the positive as you align yourself with your goal. "Bad luck" comes from just the opposite use of your energy and the rest of your life forces. (Fortunately, because of my alignment, I was the recipient of very good luck!)

When you're in the state of "The Alignment," you're living in the positive, a state of active, constructive hope. You're consciously endorsing a brilliant present and a brilliant future and things just seem to go your way. You're always in the right place at the right time. The Universe really is working with you to help make your dreams come true. Your vision is very powerful; it's the living image of your heart's inspiration and motivating force. Often, more than we're consciously aware of, it wants and needs to come to fruition.

Pay attention to the signs along your path as you journey toward success. Notice what shows up and when and how it shows up. In the movie, "Bruce Almighty," Jim Carrey's character has had a hard day and while aimlessly driving around that night, he prayed out loud for guidance. He repeatedly asked for a "sign" so that he'd know what to do. Suddenly, from his left—the spiritual, intuitive, inspirational side—a municipal truck pulled in front of him. The truck was transporting various road signs, "*Wrong Way*", "*Yield*", "*Stop,*" and others with similar messages.

Bruce chose to ignore the messages the signs gave him because they weren't the type of signs he was expecting, so of course, he wound up in an avoidable, horrendous but comic accident. This is my favorite scene in the movie because it illustrates its message so clearly—the signs offering you the help you want and need don't always come the way you expect them to, but they always come right on time. If you're perceptive and aware of what's going on in your environment, you'll be able to recognize when a "sign" appears and what it's telling you.

Two essential factors necessary to be able to benefit from "The Alignment" are listening and gratitude. The ability to listen is much more than just being able to hear. Hearing is a physical attribute, it fulfills the auditory function in your body's communication system. It's not something you have to think about, you do it automatically.

True listening, being able to discern the meanings of the internal as well as external "signs" or messages you receive, requires a deeper, more conscious action. It's a natural attribute, as well as a developed skill. It fulfills the function of connecting to Source in your soul's communication system. To truly listen means to hear, sense and feel what is being communicated on all levels—the physical, the mental, the spiritual and the emotional. It involves paying attention to and using your intuition (sometimes called hunches or 'gut feelings'). To truly listen, get the message being conveyed and take the action called for, means you have to have faith and trust when there is often no outward "proof" that you're receiving correct information.

Gratitude, the state of being thankful and expressing that thankfulness is immeasurable in value. It's the energy that cements relationships and melts resistance while at the same time enabling all of the parties involved to have a rich, deep, meaningful, spiritually connected experience. Remember to thank those you connect with for the help they give you; remember to thank the Universe (also known as God, Higher Power and Divine Energy among other names); and remember to thank yourself.

In addition to feeling empowered, I was also beginning to feel the kind of excitement that comes with knowing that, even though the race had just started, I was going to win. My competitive adrenalin juices had kicked in and I was flying! My vision and I were one! All I had to do was stick to the steps on the list, listen to my intuition and keep moving in the right direction. I was a witness to and a participant in making magic and miracles happen and I loved it!

Pretty exciting, isn't it? That's how I felt, too. I had to remind myself that I couldn't operate from an emotional space, though. It's important to keep in mind, no matter how excited you get, you'll need to keep your feet on the ground and continue to put one foot in front of the other as you march forward on one of the most exhilarating journeys of your life.

Here, in this step, you'll often be required to set aside your emotions and with clarity and courage, objectively sort through the information and sources you've gathered and assess your progress in achieving your vision. The necessity for clarity and objectivity are obvious, but why do you need courage? You'll need courage because you'll have to be impartial—unemotional, detached—as you assess the information you've gathered and the people you've encountered, as well as the new options or perspectives that are likely to present themselves to you as you go about pursuing your goal. Remember, this is your dream. You want it to successfully come together.

Dreams and visions, by the very nature of their being, are emotionally based desires. They come from and are powerfully connected to your heart, the birthplace of all emotions. Sometimes our desire for a particular outcome is so strong that we can delude ourselves into making the wrong choices—the choices that fit our desired outcome. It takes courage to be impartial enough to tell yourself the truth about the actual value of each bit of information you collect and each person you encounter on your quest.

No matter how you feel about your dream or vision, the people you've gathered to help you or the information you've acquired, you may need to make changes, adjust your plans, bring in new people and energy and let go of the old ones if they're not working. This isn't always easy, especially if you don't have or don't know what will replace them, yet. If you find yourself in this situation, it's tempting and very natural at this stage to have doubts about whether you've got what it takes or if your dream was ever meant to come true.

Experiencing doubt, temporarily lacking confidence or wanting to give into fear are all issues or "passages" you may have to deal with and go through on your journey. Don't get stuck in one of these quagmires. Keep moving and you'll get through them! Find someone you can talk to, someone who will listen and allow you to express—and sometimes, vent—your frustration, doubts and fears as well as your hopes about your project. It's times like this that your support system comes in handy. Call on your mentor, support group and/or life coach. Talk with one or all of them. You may not come away from this venting session with any new information, but you'll come away with something just as valuable, a sense of relief and release because you're not weighed down with mental and emotional clutter any more. What often follows that sense of relief and release is a clearer perspective, accompanied by fresh inspiration and ideas.

One of the most important and valuable skills you'll develop during this stage of the process is learning how to "wait productively." Though blessed with opposable thumbs and the ability to make choices, we humans don't do the "patience" thing very well. In almost every religion and spiritual discipline, patience—the ability to wait well—is stressed. The quote by Piers Plowman, *"Patience is a virtue,"* sums it up beautifully. The reason we don't do waiting very well is because we're afraid that what we want and have to wait for, won't happen. Waiting productively, whether it's for two minutes or two years, requires what I call the *"five letter words"*– faith and trust.

Be productive, use your waiting time well. While you're waiting for people to return your calls, things you've started in motion to reach a particular point, or any of the myriad things that come up when you're making "magic" happen, sit with the ideas you're developing and the results you've attained so far. See your project from all angles as you impartially contemplate your next step. Take the time "between times" to assess your support system of people, sources and information and their willingness or ability to help you accomplish your goal.

It's also especially important at this time for you to reassess the depth of your commitment. You've taken your vision to the "real world" and now you're very likely encountering "real world" issues, many of them outside your power to control, like the often frustrating occurrences of delays, blocks and disappointments.

When something is delayed or blocked, resulting in your having to wait, there is almost always a benefit for you in this seemingly stopped flow of energy, depending on how you look at it. When you're traveling along the highway and you encounter a detour sign that redirects you—technically, you've been blocked from proceeding as planned and possibly delayed as a result. That's one way to look at it.

You could also look at it this way—if you're prevented from going in the direction you'd planned and redirected to a different route—you'll have a chance to see different sites, meet new people, encounter varied scenery and get a new perspective on your journey. That's what a delay or a block offers you, an opportunity to see and experience different things as well as an opportunity to see and experience familiar things from a different perspective.

If you approach life's inevitable delays and blocks with an openness and an expectation of learning something new from the experience, your positive energy flow won't be bogged down by anger or frustration and you'll very often be pleased by what you discover on the new route.

One of the gnarlier truths about life is, at some point there will be disappointments. Sometimes, no matter what the weather forecaster promises—it's going to rain on your parade. The same holds true for people and the promises they make and for whatever reason, don't keep. It doesn't matter how much they love you or promise to be there for you, there will be those instances when they just don't show up for you. And there's no denying that that hurts. You can't really do anything about the "rain" or the broken promises, but there is something you can do about the way you handle those circumstances. If you let the disappointments and the disappointers define you and your dream, then, you'll have given your power to them. If you persevere despite the disappointments or set-backs, you'll not only retain your power, you'll increase it and have more confidence in yourself and more determination to make your dream come true.

There is an old saying, *"Translate your pain into purpose."* When affected by forces like these that are beyond your immediate control, realize that you've been presented with an excellent opportunity to transmute and direct the painful energy of disappointment into an energy that's far more powerful, purposeful and productive.

Although it can feel very personal when someone goes back on their word, in most cases, it isn't. Please do your best to maintain your balance and not take it personally (even if, at first, you might—you're human, after all). If you do find yourself taking it personally—don't get stuck in negative feelings! Feel your feelings, don't stuff them, but don't act on them either. No matter how things appear to be, use the energy of the pain and disappointment to move beyond what you'll later realize is only a small bump on your path. At times like this, keep in mind another old saying, *"What doesn't kill you, makes you stronger."*

The great gifts of Step 4 are organization, support and opportunities to deal with "what is" (sometimes referred to as 'reality'). All of your options are laid out in clear view so that you can see who and what you want and need to work with, i.e., what your tools are and who your helpers will be. Knowing your plan, as well as who and what are a part of your team, helps you stay focused and remain grounded as you begin to manifest your vision in the physical world. Your desire to create your vision is out in the "real world" now and like everyone and everything else here in the "real world," your vision will experience the ups and downs of the life process as it moves forward towards fruition. And just like the rest of us, with the right guidance, it'll arrive a winner and so will you.

Work Book Exercises

*"Do not wait to strike till the iron is hot;
but make it hot by striking."*
—William B. Sprague

1. Listen to *Stage 2– Steps 4 through 6* of the Guided Imagery meditation that comes with this book. Listening to this Guided Imagery meditation 15 minutes every day will help strengthen your determination and build your confidence as you continue the process of manifesting your vision. It will also help you connect your intuitive, creative, generating energy (feminine) to your intellectual, methodical, activating energy (masculine) which will heighten your level of magnetism and attract to you all manner of good luck, opportunities and helpful people and circumstances.

2. Before you go to bed, sit quietly for 15-20 minutes and listen to meditation music. Doing so will help you to more powerfully assimilate the experiences of your day and on an inner level, keep the center of creativity and desire—your heart chakra—open.

3. **Who's On Board?** Go over the "Steps Necessary to Complete My Goal" instruction guide and make a list of the types of support/help you'll need and the names, phone numbers, e-mail addresses and physical addresses of the individuals and/or groups who can help you. Be sure and write down how you think they can be of help to you (knowing and being able to articulate what you want from them will really help determine if they are the right "team" members for you and your project). Contact them and arrange to meet with them, either in person or via phone. After each meeting, make brief notes on the meeting—what was discussed, if the person committed to helping you, how they offered and/or agreed to do so, your feelings about them and the meeting. Making and keeping records of your meetings will be of great help to you. The people you meet with and those who become part of your "team" are important resources and should be catalogued for easy reference and accessibility.

4. **"To Do" & "It's Done":** This is one of the most important aids you'll create. List and review what's been accomplished so far and what still needs to be done in order of importance. This list has two main advantages, <u>1</u>- you'll be able to easily see what you've done and what still has to be done every step of the way; and <u>2</u>—the psychological and emotional boost to your self-confidence as you complete each item on the list, knowing you're one step closer to achieving your vision. And yes, you will be adding to the list from time to time. Things change and you'll be called upon to acknowledge and adjust to the changes. Once you've completed something on your list, don't erase the item, just draw a line through it. That way, every time you look at the list, you'll have the psychological satisfaction of seeing and knowing that you've completed an item and that you're one step closer to your goal.

5. **Ah—expenses!** What is your budget? Just as with all ventures, you'll need to know how much your project will cost. Gas, carfare, phone calls, paper, printer ink—all of the small as well as large expenses that you'll need to take into account if you're going to keep your "vision mission" afloat and moving forward. Estimate and itemize your projected costs and add 15% for unexpected expenditures. Keep a detailed accounting of your money (and time) spent and you'll appreciate your efforts even more, plus, you'll be less likely to be caught off guard by an unanticipated expense at an inconvenient time.

6. It's important to express gratitude. Expressing gratitude is more than just giving thanks. In addition to being an acknowledgement, it's also, to quote the author, Robert Emmons, *"a felt sense of wonder, thankfulness, and appreciation for life."* Gratitude places you in a state of grace and energetically positions you to be a magnet for the good you want to attract. Express gratitude to yourself for getting to this first stage of completion of your project. Express gratitude for the people, experiences, and blessings that have assisted you in getting to this point. And if it's an appropriate reference for you, express gratitude to the Universe or your Higher Power for all of the inspiration and courage that have been, is being and will be given to you.

Chapter 5

The number "5" is a communication, transition
and "how to" number.
It relates to changes, perceptions and perspectives, as well as the
choices that need to be made and the chances or risks that need to
be taken in any enterprise. An impartial, pivotal number, it's also a
social, boundary-less number as it calls for resolving and connecting
questions and problems to answers and solutions found through
interacting with a wide array of sources.

**This is the half-way point in achieving your goal. It's a multi-faceted stage with many different aspects, the awareness of which
are all important to the successful process of creation. Here, you'll
learn the value of shifting your perspective and how to gain from
and flow with the changes—expected and unexpected—that
naturally occur in the creation process, as well as the power and
nature of change, habits and the ego.**

*"Discovery consists in seeing what everyone else has seen and
thinking what no one else has thought."*
—Albert Szent-Gyorgyi

You're now at the point where you must work in conjunction
with other people, other concepts and other opinions. This is
always a risky place for any creator—to "go public" with your
vision. Suppose the people you tell about it don't think it's a
good idea? Or they think you're foolish, crazy and/or just wasting
your time trying to make something impossible (from their
perspective) happen? And suppose some or all of that "raining on
your parade" brings you crashing down to earth, feeling *"What's the
use?"* about your vision? Or what if, despite what anyone else has to
say about it, supportive or unsupportive, you begin to doubt
yourself or the viability of your dream?

Actually, it's rare that one or all of those things don't happen when a person begins to share their dream with the world because those are pretty standard reactions to anything new. Remember that you're seeing something that no one else is capable of seeing yet. Their minds and eyes haven't adjusted to the new vistas that you and your vision have presented to them. They don't have a language—verbal or visual—to express, understand or clearly see what you're talking about.

Although other's opinions can be helpful, even necessary, as you pursue your goal, don't fall prey to the internal and external "naysayers" and their toxic lack of vision. Naysayers live in as small and controlled a world as possible, ever fearful of anything new or different because of the expansiveness it may bring into their tiny little worlds.

Ultimately, what others think or don't think about your vision, whether they agree with you or not isn't for you to lose energy over by dwelling on them and their reasons for being negative about you and what you want to achieve. If they don't get it or you, don't waste your energy trying to convince them. Leave them in their tiny little world and continue on with making your dream a concrete reality.

Sometimes, some of the people you tell about your dream will get it and encourage you. When that happens, value the support and feel nurtured by it. Generally, though, the inability of others to see what you're seeing is pretty much par for the course and that's not your fault. Although you may want to share your vision with others, it isn't your responsibility to make them see what you're able to see. If you take on that task, for the most part, you'll be wasting your time and energy trying to convince the doubters and fearers that there is a new window through which to view the world. Remember, a sad but important truth you'll learn to accept is very well put by the dynamic motivational speaker, Les Brown, *"Those who can't see it for themselves, can't see it for you, either."*

And, yes, sometimes it might even be you who's raining on your own parade, filling your head and heart with doubts. If that happens, just remember that although you're beginning to "speak and understand" the language of your vision, you aren't fluent in it, yet. Remind yourself of the endless possibilities before you as well as all of the modern conveniences that now make our lives so comfortable that were once considered crazy, impossible or blasphemous. (When it was first introduced, the umbrella was considered a tool of the devil because it protected the person using it from the rain, which God had made!)

In addition to Columbus and his three leaky boats, there are plenty of instances of people "just not getting it." Here are a few of my favorites:

- A few years ago, the day after an actress won an Academy Award, her very conservative parents appeared on a morning television show. When the interviewer asked them if they were proud of their daughter for achieving one of American filmdom's highest honors, they very dourly replied, *"She needs to come back home and finish college so that she can get a teaching degree and settle down with a real job."*

- When Alexander Graham Bell demonstrated his new invention—the telephone—to President Rutherford B. Hayes in 1876, the president commented, "An amazing invention—but who would ever want to use one?"

- In 1948, computers were huge behemoths, about the size of an apartment block, and had to be operated by very tech-savvy specialists. Thomas J. Watson, president of IBM, could only envision a limited market for them. He very famously said, *"I think there is a world market for about five computers."* (Aren't you glad no one paid attention to that limiting pronouncement?)

Choosing to continue manifesting your vision takes a lot of something you already have—courage. It may not be obvious to you and you may have to dig deeply in order to connect to it, but it's there.

The courage, focus and determination that we need to pursue our dreams and "put them before the masses" is inherent in all of us. We all started out the same way—a generator (female) egg and an activator (male) sperm. All mammals began the great journey that would eventually lead us to birth and life at the end of the gestation period the same way—by literally braving the elements and beating the competition as the activator sperm swam upstream in order to achieve its goal of connecting with the generator egg. The single, simple sperm that won just went for it. If something got in the way, it went around it. If another sperm sped past it, it increased its determination and speed and pulled ahead of it. That single, simple sperm didn't let anything stop it as it swam for all it was worth to reach and activate that egg. The focus, determination and patience of that egg and the focus, determination and courage of that sperm resulted in YOU.

You are a result of focused, determined, courageous, patient action. These attributes are a natural part of all us—they're encoded in every part of our being. With such a focused, determined start, how could we not be winners!?

The great writer-philosopher, Ralph Waldo Emerson spoke to and for all of us when he wrote "Risk." It speaks perfectly to that part of the human psyche that evolves only when it dares to reach beyond its known set of boundaries and strives to become what we are meant to be.

> *"To risk is to risk appearing the fool.*
> *To weep is to risk appearing sentimental.*
> *To expose feelings is to risk exposing your true self.*
> *To place your ideas, your dreams, before the crowd is to risk loss.*
> *To love is to risk not being loved in return.*
> *To live is to risk dying. To try at all is to risk failure.*
> *But to risk we must.*
> *Because the greatest hazard in life is to risk nothing.*
> *The man, the woman, who risks nothing, does nothing, has nothing, is nothing."*

I repeat—it's a natural part of the creation process for questions and doubts to come up. The key to your success at this stage is learning how to deal with them so that you can turn those questions and doubts into solutions and certainty. How? By shifting your perspective and flowing with the energy of the changes, expected and unexpected, that naturally occur whenever there is an opportunity for growth. And by forging a series of powerful alliances—the first and most important alliance being you with your vision. Belief in yourself and your dream is the foundation and catalyst that changes your vision from a desire in your heart, an idea in your mind and words on a page as you apply the physical actions that will take them to the next level of creativity—the physical realm. The alliances you form with your helpers—partners, information sources, support groups—can then assist you in building the structure that is your actualized dream.

The first time I announced to my Tuesday night meditation class that we would all be embarking on this exciting adventure, I had to navigate its terrain mostly by intuition, with a healthy sprinkling of life experience, observation and student feedback.

One of my students, Abby, a home-maker and soccer mom, was the first to speak up and excitedly tell all of us what her great adventure would be. She declared that she'd always wanted to learn to raise orchids and that this course would be perfect to get her out of the 'wanting to' phase and into the 'doing' phase.

She pulled a newspaper ad from her purse that she'd torn from that day's paper announcing the formation of a new orchid growing class at one of the local nurseries and happily chirped about there being no coincidences in life. She was so enthusiastic as she spoke about the beauty, strength and frailty of this exotic flower that I found myself wanting to tag along with her to the classes.

Our homework between that class session and the next was to create the "Steps Necessary to Complete My Goal" instruction guide and make a list of the types of support and help necessary to successfully bring our dream to fruition. I was excited to find out what each student would create and bring to the class.

The following Tuesday, at the start of class, Abby again was the first to raise her hand and read her "Steps Necessary to Complete My Goal" instruction guide and support list to the class. Before reading, though, she announced that she'd changed her mind—she no longer wanted to raise orchids—she now wanted to learn about finance and investment so that she could take the control of her family's stock portfolio away from their financial advisor. Although she had no real understanding of what that would entail, she thought she'd be able to do a better job than their current advisor.

"*Oh*," I said, as I managed to keep all expression off my face. Though intelligent and strong-willed, the only job she'd held since graduating from college had been the combined one of corporate wife, homemaker and mom. Although her expertise at that multi-tasking position spoke highly of her qualifications, I wasn't sure it was enough to successfully carry her through something as complex and vital as the investment arena. As I gently asked the necessary probing questions as to how she'd made that decision and how she planned to go about it, I couldn't help thinking that Abby might be getting in over her head.

While she was answering my questions, the logical, earth bound part of me was afraid and wanted to tell her that her new goal was a very big one and would be too much for her; that she was better suited to raising orchids and pursuing her hobby, quilting. The intuitive, adventurous part of me was intrigued, though, and confidently felt that her new quest was one that was well worth whatever efforts and risks she'd meet on her new path.

As her guide and teacher, I knew I had to help Abby make a decision that would serve her as well as all of us in the class. I couldn't forbid her to change projects, but I could try to discourage her by telling her how unqualified she was to take on something as important, intricate and intense as her family's financial well being.

I carefully listened as I weighed her words and what I knew was really true about her. Finally my right brain and my left brain were in sync and I told her the only thing I could have told her at that time, "OK–go for it."

Abby's decision to change her mind and choose a different project and my intuitive sense that, despite appearances, she would prevail, are one of the clearest experiences I've ever had of the need to be willing to shift perspective and flow with the energy of the changes that can present themselves whenever we're in pursuit of our vision. What I recognized in Abby was a deep and very grounded belief in herself and her ability to achieve her vision. And that's what my senses responded to. All I had to do was be open and be willing to shift in the direction of the new changes. She was so aligned with her vision that I felt it and I had faith in her, the ideas she expressed and the determination she showed. I didn't know if she *would* be successful, but I definitely knew that she had everything she needed and *was* everything she needed to be in order to *be* successful in her quest.

By listening to your intuition, taking appropriate action, being confident (or when you have to—acting as if you are) in the face of uncertainty—yours and/or others—and having the courage of your convictions as you present your ideas to the world, you'll learn to effectively deal with whatever changes and adjustments present themselves to you.

Emerson's "Risk" is the perfect accompaniment for Step 5 because it reminds us that we're all human with our doubts and fears and that we can reawaken and reengage that part of us that is divine whenever we move beyond our self-imposed limitations and dare to be what we were meant to be—great. The simple truth is, between the time you commit to your vision and you complete it, doubts and fears are going to rear their annoyingly scary little heads more than once. The trick to winning this struggle lies in not letting these energy vampires drain you of your enthusiasm for your vision.

Change is a natural and important aspect of life. You're going to have to make different choices, adjustments and changes to your original plan. Like a tree in a windstorm, your vision will survive intact if you choose the stance of "firm flexibility"—staying grounded in your determination and shifting your attitude and approach to resolving the issues that present themselves as problems or obstacles.

The concept of change is a lofty one. Accepting it, going with it and embracing it is urged upon us by the 'wisest of the wise'— politicians, spiritual teachers and advisors of all kinds, including Moms, Dads and the next door neighbors. However, actually doing it is an entirely different matter. It's generally a case of "the spirit is willing, but the flesh is weak" when it comes time to do what's required to improve your situation by operating differently so that you get a desired outcome.

Why is that?

From what I've observed and experienced, there are four main reasons we resist change.

- **Habit.** We are creatures of habit. As creatures of habit, we allow all sorts of people and circumstances to take up residence in our lives. Who doesn't know someone who complains about an unhappy relationship but won't do anything to change their circumstances because, even though they're in pain because of the unhappy relationship, they're used to it?

- **The unknown.** We fear the unknown. Change requires us to trust and face the fact that we don't know for sure what will happen next. Everyone knows someone who's stuck in a job they don't like or aren't inspired by, but won't do anything about because they're afraid of encountering something new in their lives. The old saying, *"It's better to stick with the devil you know than to deal with the devil you don't know,"* is their motivation. If we make changes, will we make mistakes? Maybe—it's a natural part of the life/creative process. Whether we move or stay stuck, mistakes are going to happen—it's what we do about them that determines our character and our outcome. After all, most pencils come from the factory with attached erasers. The pencil manufacturers knew their customers were going to make mistakes that would need to be corrected when they made the pencils. And so did you; that's why you bought those eraser equipped pencils to begin with.

- **The power we give to our egos.** The ego is a powerful servant, but a terrible master and if we give it too much power, it will run and often ruin our lives. Changing anything requires us to admit that we aren't perfect, that we don't always know everything at the outset, that we could somehow be wrong. The ego hates admitting it's wrong or doesn't know something and will do anything—and I do mean anything—to keep from admitting it. A controlling ego is a destructive ego. You don't have to look far to find an example of a controlling ego. They're everywhere, even sometimes, in you.

- **Laziness.** This trait is stagnation's great ally. Changing anything requires some type of conscious energy output. Changing your mind requires you to be mindful of the way you gather and process information. Changing your habits requires you to move and stretch in new ways. Changing anything requires work and even the most industrious person has to consciously work at reminding themselves to leave old habits, plans and belief systems and adopt new, more beneficial ones that are consistent with achieving new goals.

Resistance to making necessary changes and refusal to make them will sink your project. All sorts of erroneous "really good reasons" why you can't, don't have to or shouldn't have to make changes you're being faced with will come up for you. If you heed them, these "really good reasons" will prop up your resistance to changing your perspective and undermine you as you pursue your goal.

John Kenneth Galbraith said it best, *"Faced with the choice between changing one's mind and proving that there is no need to do so, almost everyone gets busy on the proof."* If you find yourself busy proving that you don't need to shift, adjust or change your strategy when you're faced with the possibility of change—ask yourself if it's you talking or if it's your ego, fear and/or laziness that's causing your resistance.

Work Book Exercises

*"It's not the size of the dog in the fight,
it's the size of the fight in the dog."*

—Mark Twain

1. Listen to *Stage 2– Steps 4 through 6* of the Guided Imagery meditation that comes with this book. Listening to this Guided Imagery meditation 15 minutes every day will help strengthen your determination and build your confidence as you continue the process of manifesting your vision. It will also help you connect your intuitive, creative, generating energy (feminine) to your intellectual, methodical, activating energy (masculine) which will heighten your level of magnetism and attract to you all manner of good luck, opportunities and helpful people and circumstances.

2. Before you go to bed, sit quietly for 15-20 minutes and listen to meditation music. Doing so will help you to more powerfully assimilate the experiences of your day and on an inner level, keep the center of creativity and desire—your heart chakra—open.

3. Print "Risk" out and post it on the mirrors in your home, your refrigerator, your desk, the inside of your entry doors—even your car's dashboard and be sure to read it every chance you get. It'll be a constant support and reminder to you as you pursue your goals. You'll find this amazing declaration in the Affirmations section in the Appendix at the back of this book.

4. To paraphrase Einstein, *"You can't solve a problem with the same thinking that created it."* When the pioneering aviator, Bessie Coleman, an American black woman in the 1920's, wanted to become a pilot, she couldn't find anyone in the US willing to teach her because of her gender and race. So, she learned to speak French, went to France, found a flight instructor there and became the first person of color to earn an international pilot's license. When renowned financier, J. P. Morgan, needed

important investment information that his left-brain Wall Street advisors couldn't supply, he wisely consulted astrologers and successfully followed their advice all the way to the bank. When an applicant to the nation's top military academy was denied entry because he was half an inch too short, he didn't let that stop him. Determined to attend the academy, he researched the body's ability to transform and did stretching exercises for several months before he re-applied to the academy. With his second application, he was accepted because he had stretched his body so much that he measured a quarter of an inch taller than the lower end of the academy's height requirements!

The point is—sometimes, you need to think outside of the box. When the need to change perspectives and/or tactics presents itself to you, sit down with a pen and paper and imagine yourself in their shoes as you ask *"What would Bessie or J. P. or a height challenged military cadet do?"* and write down whatever comes to mind. This stream of consciousness thinking will allow for all sorts of innovative ideas to come to you. Thinking outside of the box liberates and has the potential to empower you as you expose yourself to new sources, information and energy. After all, when one door closes, another one will open somewhere.

5. This is one of my favorite "dispel all personal doubts and fears" exercises. I've recommended it in earlier chapters because it works so well in different circumstances. Whenever you find yourself becoming overwhelmed with self-doubt and/or fearing that you've no reason or right to expect your dreams to come true, take a pen and paper and write down your doubts and/or fears. Keep it short—two or three words will do for each doubt or fear. When you've finished your list, do what you do with all garbage—get rid of it! If you have a shredder, shred the list, put the pieces in a bag and toss the garbage into a dumpster. If you don't have a shredder, tear the list into tiny pieces, put the pieces in a bag and leave that bag of non-entities in a dumpster. Afterwards, those feelings of distress you were dealing with will be gone and you'll be in touch with your personal power again.

6. It's important to express gratitude. Expressing gratitude is more than just giving thanks. In addition to being an acknowledgement, it's also, to quote the author, Robert Emmons, *"a felt sense of wonder, thankfulness, and appreciation for life."* Gratitude places you in a state of grace and energetically positions you to be a magnet for the good you want to attract. Express gratitude to yourself for getting to this first stage of completion of your project. Express gratitude for the people, experiences, and blessings that have assisted you in getting to this point. And if it's an appropriate reference for you, express gratitude to the Universe or your Higher Power for all of the inspiration and courage that have been, is being and will be given to you.

Chapter 6

The number "6" is an assessment of value and progress number. It represents the second stage of completion of any endeavor and it involves balance, evaluation and progressive results. An editing, "prototype" or successful test run number, it relates to actual evidence of the profitable potential of an idea. It's an outward or physical encouragement stage that indicates victory and points out the rewards that can be had from your vision.

You have now reached the second stage of completion of your project. Here is where you really begin to see the probable profit that can be had from your vision and your efforts to manifest it. Things will start to flow more smoothly from here on because you have actual (physical) proof of what your finished project will look or be like. This stage points to the possibilities and manifestation of powerful support and possible partnerships and investment in you and your idea. You'll learn the value of sorting and arranging priorities as you position your project to be viewed and appreciated by the world.

"The question is not what you look at, but what you see."
—Henry David Thoreau

This is an important stage of development for you. You have achieved something: a victory that reflects the efforts you've put into making your vision a concrete reality. Victory is a marvelous word. Say it out loud—*"Victory!"* As it rolls off your tongue, it automatically confers a sense of self-confidence, a feeling that encourages you to trust yourself and fearlessly move forward, regardless of what anyone else may think.

This stage of development is the appreciation stage. There are so many different ways its root word, appreciate, can be used. One is as an expression of gratitude—"*I really appreciate your help,*" another is an evaluation —"*the painting will appreciate in value,*" and a third is to exercise wise judgment and keen insight in realizing or determining worth—"*we can appreciate their work ethic.*"

All three uses of "*appreciate*" apply to you and your progress at this point. By acknowledging and expressing gratitude to yourself, the people who've helped you get to this point and to your spiritual source, you're strengthening the connection between you and all of the creative forces in life. You're literally telling them that you're all on the same team and you want them to continue participating with you as you work to make your vision a reality.

The evaluation aspect of "*appreciate*" is a win-win for you. Your positive and profitable actions have resulted in something of value and as you continue to develop your vision, that value will increase and deepen in ways that you could never have previously predicted. You will literally be living and benefiting from this part of William Hutchinson Murray's great quote—"*All sorts of things occur to help one that would never otherwise have occurred. A whole system of events issues from the decision—raising in one's favor all manner of unforeseen incidents and meetings and material assistance—which no one could have ever dreamed would have come one's way.*"

The third aspect of "*appreciate*" is so simple and so great—your "stock" in yourself will go up. Your sense of self-worth will automatically be elevated by just seeing what you've done so far. Your direct experience and knowledge that you can take the intangible; a hope, a wish or a dream from the ethereal realm of desire and transform it into something that has a tangible presence in your life is priceless and will only increase in value. From this point on, nothing and no one will ever be able to convince you that you can't create miracles!

Remember the theme quote for this chapter? "*The question is not what you look at, but what you see.*"

In this, the "will it fly" stage, there is still work to be done, but it's now the work of a more detailed refinement of the physical manifestation of your project. In the clothing design world, we call this stage, the "muslin" stage; in the theatre, it's called the dress rehearsal stage. A muslin is the design that started out as an idea, became a two-dimensional sketch and is now the first three-dimensional version of the actual garment, usually, though not always, made out of a non-descript beige colored cloth. It's from this "proto-type" that decisions are made regarding fit, style and the garment's appeal to the buying public. And as with all muslins and prototypes, adjustments must be made. Perhaps, instead of long sleeves, the garment would work better with three-quarter length sleeves and instead of those darling pleats in the front (the idea of which inspired you to make the garment in the first place), it would fit and look better without them.

The refinement or editing stage of the development of your vision can be intense and surprisingly emotional, sometimes even painful. Aspects that you previously thought had little or no importance, begin to be seen as important and must be emphasized; conversely, aspects that may have inspired you or were originally considered essential to the success of the vision may now be considered unnecessary and will need to be eliminated.

This truthfully stated, poetically brutal observation, attributed to both playwright Tennessee Williams and Cornish writer Sir Arthur Quiller-Couch and paraphrased here—"*In the creative process, sometimes, you must be willing to murder your darlings,*" is never more deeply felt than at this stage of development. I can't tell you the number of times I struggled with the realization that eliminating a beautiful inspirational detail from a garment or a brilliantly written turn of phrase from an article or a book would make the end result better. Though beautiful, brilliant and inspiring on its own, once the garment, article or book begins to come together, that particular piece just doesn't work anymore and it must be excised for the successful outcome of the project.

That same struggle is also present when you have to add something to your original idea that you don't like or wholly agree with but will actually give your vision the viability it needs without compromising its integrity in the material realm.

This editing process is generally easier when you have the support and input of those who're more experienced in taking an idea or vision from the ethereal plane to the physical world. Even if the more experienced person doesn't have expertise in your particular field, they can still offer you a lot of helpful wisdom. Remember, you can always learn something new.

What if, though, despite the advice and despite how bulky those once darling pleats make your garment, you don't want to or you just can't give them up? This is where balance comes in. If you feel that you must push on with your original concept intact, make an agreement with yourself that if you haven't resolved the problem or achieved what you've been going for by a certain time or at a particular point in the creative process, you'll honestly reconsider your stance and approach the project in a way that'll ensure its successful completion. At the very least, you'll learn what the energy feels like as you approach and deal with the current limits of possibility. And, who knows, you may make those pleats work with that garment and achieve immeasurable satisfaction and success.

If you do decide to stick with your unaltered inspirational touches and/or concepts at this point, be aware that this method of manifestation emphasizes the "journey" as opposed to the "destination" aspect in manifesting your vision. This "unaltered" approach definitely adds more seasoning to an already spicy adventure and because of that, balance and self-honesty are the keys to making it work. Although this method is akin to white water rafting in the Rockies as opposed to team rowing on the Charles River, there is something to be said about the rush you get when you challenge the elements. This is a decision that you'll have to make. Although, I personally like a good challenge once in a while, I've come to appreciate flowing along with the natural current as I "listen" to it "tell" me how to make it go in a different or better direction.

If this all sounds a little like you're going back and forth between Step 5—perceptions, perspectives, choices and changes, and where you are now—Step 6, you're right. As you work with and refine the now physical aspect of your vision, you'll be required to be flexible as you base your decision making on how your vision is actually forming itself in the physical world. As you make each necessary change, Step 5, you'll automatically be using the energy of *"appreciation"*—evaluation, Step 6, to determine how you and your refinement process need to proceed. Don't be dismayed if the refinement stage takes a little longer than you expected. By the very nature of its definition, this can be a labor and time intensive step. You literally do have to "listen" to your "muslin" or "prototype" as you decide what details are important to its successful manifestation.

I like to build things: coats, furniture, abstract art pieces, and many a time, I've tried to walk away from having to heed the calling of a particular aspect of my project. Once, when I was making a very detail laden winter coat, after many hours of preparation, I finally attached the collar to the body of the coat. I was so relieved! I'd spent over fifteen hours just getting to that point, in addition to which, I'd wounded myself in the process when I ran my hand along the point of a forgotten pin and gouged out a fair amount of skin and flesh. Needless to say, I was pretty much over the collar by this time and wanted nothing more to do with it. At least now that it was sewn into the coat, I could move on to easier, less tedious and more instantly rewarding aspects of the coat construction. Or so I thought.

I put the coat on the dress form and stood back to admire my work. Something was wrong. The finished coat collar was one inch too wide and it threw the balance of the entire garment off! Granted, it was exactly as I'd sketched it, but, now in its three-dimensional form, I could see that the dimensions of the collar didn't work with the overall design of the coat. I could also see that the coat was beautiful and nobody else would notice that the collar was an inch too wide but me. I tried using that reasoning to convince myself that I didn't need to make any changes; that I'd grow to love the coat as it was.

It was three o'clock in the morning, I was tired, my hand was throbbing and my head hurt. I told myself that I'd see things differently after a good night's sleep and I went to bed. The next morning, after a brisk walk in the countryside and a rejuvenating deep meditation, I approached the dress form, removed the protective cloth cover, stood back and looked at the coat with fresh eyes. And with fresh eyes I saw that the coat collar was still one inch too wide. Yes, it's true that no one else would know, but I'd know and I knew I'd never be happy with the coat as long as that collar was out of proportion to the rest of the coat.

So, I surrendered to my vision and my commitment to honor it. I took the coat off the dress form, sat in a comfy chair with plenty of good light and spent the day removing the collar from the coat stitch by stitch, taking the collar apart, cutting it down, re-sewing it and re-attaching it to the coat.

Finally, as the day turned into night, my alterations were finished and I tried on the coat with its newly slenderized collar. As I looked at my reflection in the mirror, I instantly knew that I'd been right to surrender my ego and reluctance and follow the dictates of my vision and my commitment to it. Though still unfinished, the coat was beautiful, like a symphony! Not one note out of place. All of the time, energy and angst of dealing with the detail of the collar had been worth it. I still had a long way to go before completion, but I knew that my coat was not only going to keep me warm, it was going to be, to paraphrase my friend, David, *"a fitting raiment for your regal presence, bringing joy to all who gaze upon it."*

The number 6 is also a number of love, relationship and harmony. You and your vision are in a committed relationship. You have to love your vision and take the actions called for if you're going to see it through to completion. And as in any relationship, through the easy times and the difficult times, you'll have to remind yourself, time and time again, that you love it and re-commit to it. It won't always be easy but it will always be worth it.

If your vision has a more impersonal form and/or includes other people: partners, investors, teachers, sales teams, buyers, focus groups; they'll be a part of your evaluation team as you begin to introduce your project to the world. Almost every good idea can be made better with someone else's perspective. The feedback, observations and recommendations all of you make regarding your project will need to be sifted and sorted through and weighed with as much objectivity as possible in order to determine and apply meaningful value to the success of your vision. Remembering to surrender to the integrity of the vision and not the ego, is an important component of allowing this step to work for you.

"Surrender to the integrity of the vision and not the ego"—what does that mean?

Simply put, it means that in all discussions and decisions regarding your vision, please keep in mind that you and your team have gotten together for a common goal. And that goal is the essence, the heart, the integrity—the spiritual center of your vision and what you want to accomplish. Remember, as you're refining your project, you may have good ideas, but often, they can be improved upon with someone else's input. Rather than let your ego convince you that you, your opinion, experience or anything else is being disregarded or disrespected, remember that you and the other person or people have gotten together to further something much bigger than the ego's feeling slighted because someone else has a different viewpoint. You have all gotten together to make your dream come true. This doesn't mean you have to tolerate meanness, instability or disrespect; it does mean that, regardless of your feelings about anything, you must keep things in perspective and make your decisions for the greater good of your vision from this objective stance.

Work Book Exercises

"Our grand business in life is not to see what lies dimly at a distance, but to do what lies clearly at hand."
—Thomas Carlyle

1. Listen to *Stage 2– Steps 4 through 6* of the Guided Imagery meditation that comes with this book. Listening to this Guided Imagery meditation 15 minutes every day will help strengthen your determination and build your confidence as you continue the process of manifesting your vision. It will also help you connect your intuitive, creative, generating energy (feminine) to your intellectual, methodical, activating energy (masculine) which will heighten your level of magnetism and attract to you all manner of good luck, opportunities and helpful people and circumstances.

2. Before you go to bed, sit quietly for 15-20 minutes and listen to meditation music. Doing so will help you to more powerfully assimilate the experiences of your day and on an inner level, keep the center of creativity and desire—your heart chakra—open.

3. It's important to express gratitude. Expressing gratitude is more than just giving thanks. In addition to being an acknowledgement, it's also, to quote the author, Robert Emmons, *"a felt sense of wonder, thankfulness, and appreciation for life."* Gratitude places you in a state of grace and energetically positions you to be a magnet for the good you want to attract. Express gratitude to yourself for getting to this second stage of completion of your goal. Express gratitude for the people, experiences, and miracles that have assisted you in getting to this point. And if it's an appropriate reference for you, express gratitude to the Universe or your Higher Power for all of the inspiration, courage and good fortune that continue to accompany you on your journey.

4. Make a list of what needs to be altered at this point in the creation of your vision. Edit and amend your original Commitment Statement and "Steps to Complete My Goal" instruction guide to reflect the necessary changes.

5. Celebrate your progress and results up to this point. Acknowledge yourself and how far you've come and what it's taken to get here. Relax and spend some time admiring the process, the project, your support and yourself. As frivolous and time consuming as this exercise may seem to some—its gifts to you are invaluable. Every living thing thrives on acknowledgement. In almost every circumstance, when we're acknowledged for our time and participation in something, that acknowledgement has the magical effect of encouraging, enlivening and energizing us.

6. Buy yourself a present. It doesn't have to be expensive, it just has to be meaningful to you. This is a great way to have a conscious reminder of your expressing gratitude to yourself. Every time you see it, you'll think of this step and it'll remind you that you have created something of value as it encourages you to continue on and complete your project.

Chapter 7

The number "7" is both an intuition number and
an intellect number.
It relates to a need for powerful self-trust and a need to be aware of,
listen to and logically use the information your intuition provides
you with. It refers to competitive forces, your other ideas and/or
methods as well as other people's ideas and/or methods. It speaks
of the need to seek out, trust and follow the advice of experts,
which includes Divine Guidance. It also represents convincing the
masses and/or person or persons of power to see the value of your
project or vision so that they fully support it and you.

**At this stage, you're nearly ¾ of the way toward the successful
completion of your vision. (Interestingly enough, it's at this stage
that many people abandon their projects!) It's here that you must
combine the power of your intuition and what I call the "5 letter
words"—faith and trust—with strategy in order to correctly
position your project in the most favorable light.**

*"When you let intuition have its way with you, you open
up new levels of the world. Such opening-up is the
most practical of all activities."*
—Evelyn Underhill

N ow that you can actually see the viability of your vision and
you've given yourself, your vision and those who support
you a high five, it's time to take another look at your
project and its target audience, as well as your supporters and your
competition.

It's natural to experience many changes in the pursuit of
manifesting your vision. Your target audience may have changed;

your vision may have changed; your supporters may have changed; you may have changed.

"What could change any or all of these elements as I make my way to success?"

The ever evolving process of growth and life and your new-found level of self-awareness that comes as a result of courageously expanding your life by manifesting your vision, that's what! Life and all it encompasses is organic, meaning we are constantly evolving, growing, becoming. Even if we sit and do nothing, we are always on every level, by the very nature of our being, changing. Though we can't control the process of organic change, we can certainly have a guiding hand in it to a desired outcome or destination by taking charge of how we use our energy and our opportunities.

If your quest is a personal goal, then you are your target audience **and** your competition. "My *own* competition!" you might be saying, "*How can that be!?*" Competition is another interesting word that is only partially explained and understood. One of Webster's Dictionary definitions for competition is *"the rivalry or struggle among elements or organisms for dominance or survival."* You don't need to engage an outside force or person to be in a competitive relationship. In the world of ideas, being of two or more minds about something automatically creates a type of rivalry or struggle for dominance of one of those ideas.

By Step 7, there are usually so many diverse ways you can make choices and so many different decisions you can make about the various options that your quest has revealed to you. All of them seem to be yelling loudly for your attention; all of them competing with one another for you to choose them.

Your intuition and your intellect, along with your experience of your quest thus far, with your intuition taking the lead and having the final say, are the tools you need to use in order to discern which of the competing choices, issues or options is most beneficial for you to decide to go with.

Another way competition shows up is by all of the ideas and differing points of view that'll naturally come up for you at this point. Sometimes it's as if your mind is a corporate boardroom during a stockholder's meeting and each thought, idea or opinion is clamoring to be recognized at the same time. If you aren't consciously aware of this inner clamoring for control of your energy and your quest, this mental "boardroom meeting" quickly hi-jacks your energy and devolves into what I call "the committee in your head having a food fight." And like any food fight, nothing is easily (if ever) resolved and you'll be left with a mess to clean up afterwards.

This potential "food fight" scenario happens to all of us at this point in pursuing a quest. It's actually a sign that you have excess energy and intuitive ability available for you to use any way you consciously choose. Remember, energy doesn't care how it's used, it simply exists to be used. If you don't consciously use it, it'll unconsciously use you. And whenever energy unconsciously uses you, the results are rarely pretty.

The best way to channel all of that unconscious clamoring for your attention is to re-direct the energy by following the advice I gave for dealing with fear in Chapter 2—get physical. By doing something that requires you to be fully engaged physically, your energy will be directed and your mind will be occupied with the form of physicality that you've chosen in a constructive way. Take a walk, clean the house, paint a room—it doesn't matter what you do as long as you consciously choose to physically use all of that excess energy. And remember to breathe big, deep, gentle, rhythmic breaths! Most people who find themselves in stressful or intense situations aren't breathing deeply at all, they're taking shallow breaths and getting just enough oxygen to keep them from passing out. The brain needs oxygen to function properly; without enough oxygen, you're likely to be as effective as a hamster on a wheel.

As you mindfully breathe deeply, gently and rhythmically and get into whatever physical task you've chosen to do, your mind begins to calm down and you start becoming aware of information and solutions that had previously eluded you. With this simple, effective method for centering yourself, you'll be able to astutely translate that new-found wealth of intuitive knowledge into a workable plan.

One of my favorite examples of this is in the 1948 Academy Award nominated classic film, "*I Remember Mama.*" When the strictly enforced hospital regulations wouldn't allow Mama to visit her hospitalized child, she did what she always did whenever she faced a problem she couldn't immediately work out—she went home and began scrubbing the floors. As she physically channeled her energy, her mind calmed, frustration no longer blinded her and she realized something—the hospital's cleaning women had free run of the facility! The next (and most moving) scene of the film shows her returning to the hospital disguised as a cleaning woman, making her way to her daughter's room and being there for her daughter when she awakens from the anesthesia.

Mama knew something that we all need to remember: getting your mental and emotional energy under your conscious control will help you to sort out any problem and come up with a winning solution.

The real key in navigating Step 7 is to position yourself, not just your project. By consciously being the physical channel of all of the energies running through you, you'll be able to position yourself so that you can "listen" intuitively and discern what action is best for you to take at any given time. In so doing, you'll be combining your experience, your intuition and your intellect and you'll know what your strategy needs to be in order to move your project into the best position for it to become the physical manifestation of your vision.

When Bria came to me for help in manifesting her vision of becoming a travel agent who specialized in naturally spectacular, off-the-beaten path get-a-ways for executive women, she knew very clearly what her motivation was. In addition to wanting to make a lot of money, she wanted to provide a service that gave over-worked women a place to gather, relax, share their stories and create a sense of like minded community. It came as a complete surprise to her that her true motivation, discovered only by going through the experience of making her vision come alive, was practically the opposite of what she'd previously thought.

Bria was her community's Yenta, the go-to person for making all things wonderful happen. From finding a rare species of tropical fish to helping someone find their perfect mate, she could be counted on to perform miracles for everyone who depended on her. And everyone: her husband, children, friends, neighbors and co-workers depended on her. So much so that, most of her 24-hour clock was devoted to the happiness of others.

It was at Step 7, at my suggestion that she try sorting through everyone else's and her own "2 cents worth" opinions about what she should do about creating her executive women's retreats and how she should do it, while doing the physical work of stocking the shelves of a neighborhood food bank, that she realized why the concept of creating a naturally spectacular, off-the-beaten path get-a-way for executive women was so appealing to her. At a naturally spectacular, off-the-beaten path get-a-way, most of the 'mod-cons' (modern conveniences) that we've gotten used to don't work, and that includes cell phones! It turned out, as Bria discovered, what she really wanted was alone time. She really wanted to be in a place where she could just be without being someone else's buddy, chauffeur or savior.

Once she became conscious of her true motivation: her own personal need to reconnect with and resource herself, she was able to position herself and her quest so that she could properly direct her energy and enlist the help she needed to make it all happen.

If your quest is a professional one, the process is very similar. Instead of just dealing with the "committee in your head," you also have to deal with all of the people, experts and fact sheets that'll weigh in on the process and progress of your project. In order to stop the boardroom shuffle and properly sort through all of the opinions and information swirling around you, you and your team need to collectively meet and put all of your concerns and issues about the project on the table. Once those concerns and issues are sorted through at the meeting, you all need to individually get physical with your actions. Each member of your team needs to notice what comes up for them, mentally and emotionally, as they focus on their individual assignments and then, after an agreed upon time, meet again and discuss the new insights and awareness's that have come up for each of you, as well as how those insights and awareness's can impact the outcome of your project.

The natural result of this process is priceless because vital information and solutions to problems that wouldn't otherwise have come to light, are now consciously available to you. Together, you and your team will be able to create an informed strategy that will move your project a big step closer to its successful completion. Just as with the personal quest, once you know your true motivation, you'll be able to present a desirable project to your target audience in a viable way that will appeal to them so much that they'll want to give you what you want, i.e., agreement, cooperation, money.

Fraternal New England twins, laid back Dave and very formal Edward (*"don't call me Ed!"*), decided to initiate their long range plan of building a hotel on the beautiful Pacific island vacation spot they loved by first opening a charter fishing business and dive shop. The island, popular with up-scale professionals, their children and serious water sports enthusiasts, was a picture perfect example of a tropical paradise come to life.

Dave and Edward did their research, drew up their plans and successfully enlisted investors who wanted to be a part of something as wonderful and potentially profitable as the twin's project.

Friendly, likable guys, they were surprised and frustrated by the official roadblocks they kept encountering as they tried to get the permits and other official permission they needed to begin the building of their version of heaven. Whenever they had a meeting with one of the island's officials to discuss their project and apply for the much needed permits, the meeting would go well from their perspective. They were always well prepared with money to pay whatever fees were required to secure the permits and their paper work was always in order. As they extolled the benefits of their project for the island's economic growth and emphasized the amount of employment that would be available for the locals, the officials always seemed enthusiastic about their plans. They'd leave the meeting feeling that they'd convinced the official and their permits would be granted within a few days.

They had at least a half dozen meetings with various island officials, always ending the same way. The official would be enthusiastic, tell them he or she would have to check with the other island officials and suggest they come back in a couple of days to fill out the necessary paperwork and pick up their permits.

And each time they went back to do the official paperwork and get their permits, they'd be told that they had to talk to a different official. When they met for the second time with the same official they'd had their first meeting with, they finally had to admit what they'd started to suspect, that they were being given the run-around.

Why they were being treated this way, they couldn't figure out. They always showed up at the appointed time, presented their plans clearly, had proof of their financial backing—they did everything they were supposed to do. What was the problem!!??

When they asked the advice of one of their friends, someone who'd grown up there and who ran the island jeep tours, she told them that she'd need some time to think about their problem and recommended that they put their plans on hold for a few days and assist her while she helped prepare for the island's annual harvest celebration. The twins were aware of the harvest celebration because they'd vacationed on the island one year when it was being held. They, like all of the other tourists, enjoyed watching as the islanders participated in their ancient harvest ceremonies.

As Dave and Edward helped their friend, Leia, she took them all over the island. They were surprised to find out there were areas of the island they'd never known were there. They met some of the older island families and shared meals with other locals as they helped dig the food roasting pits and build the covered open air dining pavilion. Although their project was never far from their minds, it wasn't the only thing they were concerned with anymore. The more work they did on the harvest celebration, the more they felt connected to the people and the spirit of the community. They even brought gifts for the local deities when it was time to dedicate the pavilion.

Working late one night to finish the celebration's preparations, they each realized how differently the islanders treated them now then they had in the past. The islanders had always been polite, but now their greetings and interactions with the twins were warm and welcoming. Dave and Edward finally understood that though they'd been respectful of the islanders, they had been insulting them by not learning about, acknowledging and honoring their culture. Of course they had trouble getting the official cooperation they needed! They'd approached the officials the way they would have in New England, with facts, figures and flowcharts. The island wasn't New England and therefore didn't operate the way New England did. Although the facts, figures and flowcharts were important to the islanders, personal connections were of even more importance to the island community. By getting physical and immersing themselves in their environment, they got out of their heads and could finally hear what their inner voice was telling them—coming from their heads in a place where coming from the heart is more valued was never going to get them the permission they wanted.

That night, as Leia drove them home, they told her about their revelation and asked her if that had been her plan all along. She didn't answer them. She didn't need to, her big smile said it all.

Patience, faith, trust, inner knowing, appropriate action. All of these words and phrases define the qualities you must embrace and strengthen at this stage of developing your vision.

1. ***Patience***–I call patience, the "P" word. *Why?* Because it's a word and an action that most of us don't want to hear or perform. When we hear it or have to practice it, it often feels like a "bad" word. But it isn't a "bad" word. Patience is another way of productively using your energy (that's probably why it's considered a virtue). There is no difference in the fifteen minutes you have to stand in line before the doors open to let you into a concert venue to hear your favorite band and the fifteen minutes you have to spend listening to a boring speech. True, one is the prelude to an enjoyable event and the other is, well, let's face it, a real drag. However, they are both the same amount of seconds and minutes. How you deal with and process your emotions is where the difference lies. The next time you're faced with the necessity to wait when you don't want to, objectively observe how your mind twists, distorts and elongates that waiting time until it becomes pure torture, and then consciously decide to experience the waiting process in a benign way. You'll find that there is a 180 degree difference in your experience of mentally torturing yourself and objectively staying centered. When you stay centered, you can see and process to your advantage, all of the information at hand.

2. ***Faith and Trust, the "5 letter words"***–Those are beautiful words, aren't they? But they suffer from the same neglect and lack of appreciation that patience does. To activate the power of faith and trust, you have to have patience. You have to believe, without physical proof, that a promise is going to be kept; that something you want to happen is going to materialize in a timely manner. The first and most important place to locate

faith and trust is within yourself. Ask yourself, *"On a scale of 1 to 10, with this project, how much do I really believe in my ability to make it happen successfully and why?"* Write your answers on the form in the work book section at the end of this chapter and then, ask yourself, *"On a scale of 1 to 10, with this project, how much do I doubt my ability to make it happen successfully and why?"* Write those answers on the form in the work book section at the end of this chapter, tpp. Next write this affirmation by Henry Ford on the form in the work book section at the end of this chapter, *"Whether you believe you can do a thing or not, you are right."* Then write your feelings and beliefs about the affirmation. The point of this exercise is simple, (1) you get to see just how much you believe in yourself and the reasons for your belief, (2) you get to see just how much you doubt yourself and the reasons for your doubts, (3) you get to decide if you're going to have faith and trust in yourself to successfully manifest your vision or if you're going to give the power of your vision to the doubts and fears that snap at the heels of every great idea, (4) you get to find out that, either way, you're going to be right. The limitless bounty of faith and trust can only be ascertained at the end result of an endeavor. You're nearly ¾ of the way there; you've come this far, why not take it all the way to completion?

3. **Inner Knowing**—*"Be still and know."* By quieting your ever active mind, you'll allow your natural intuitive source of information to express itself. Sometimes the expression comes in a flash—*"Aha!"*—sometimes it seems to float up to your consciousness from some deep well of knowledge; sometimes it comes in the form of signs or symbols. It can come in a myriad of ways. All you have to do is be able to recognize that the information is there and allow yourself to "hear" it. Practicing silent meditation and listening to guided imagery meditations are excellent ways to quiet your mind and strengthen your connection to your intuition.

4. **Appropriate action**—*What is appropriate action?* Appropriate action is simply taking the correct steps in the right way at the most optimum time to achieve a desired outcome. By properly

combining the ethereal energies of patience, faith, trust and inner knowing with the practical, physical energy of appropriate action, you'll always manifest something of value that will enhance your progress.

Work Book Exercises

"Words are also actions, and actions are a kind of words."
—Ralph Waldo Emerson

1. Listen to *Stage 3– Steps 7 through 9* of the Guided Imagery meditation that comes with this book. Listening to this Guided Imagery meditation 15 minutes every day will help strengthen your determination and build your confidence as you continue the process of manifesting your vision. It will also help you connect your intuitive, creative, generating energy (feminine) to your intellectual, methodical, activating energy (masculine) which will heighten your level of magnetism and attract to you all manner of good luck, opportunities and helpful people and circumstances.

2. Before you go to bed, sit quietly for 15-20 minutes and listen to meditation music. Doing so will help you to more powerfully assimilate the experiences of your day and on an inner level, keep the center of creativity and desire—your heart chakra— open.

3. At this point in manifesting your vision, you'll begin to notice that all kinds of impressions, doubts and related as well as unrelated ideas will try to take up residence in your mind and distract you. This is simply the result of excess energy that has no other outlet. In addition to meditating, it's important that you take time out of every day and do some mindless physical task: sort through the medicine cabinet, rearrange your sock drawer, clean off your desk. Working in the garden or going for a walk will work, too. Afterwards, when you return to working on your project, you'll find that you'll get more meaningful work done because you'll have more clarity and more control over your energy.

4. On a regular basis, meander (don't rush from exhibit to exhibit!) through the zoo, visit a botanical garden and/or spend some time in a butterfly reserve—lose yourself in nature. Don't forget, we're a natural part of life, too. By visiting these places

of natural beauty and wonder, you reconnect with the essence and majesty of life. This priceless gift of reconnection naturally invigorates and inspires you and your renewed enthusiasm will pay off in countless, often magical ways.

5. It's important to express gratitude. Expressing gratitude is more than just giving thanks. In addition to being an acknowledgement, it's also, to quote the author, Robert Emmons, *"a felt sense of wonder, thankfulness, and appreciation for life."* Gratitude places you in a state of grace and energetically positions you to be a magnet for the good you want to attract. Express gratitude to yourself for getting to this first stage of completion of your project. Express gratitude for the people, experiences, and blessings that have assisted you in getting to this point. And if it's an appropriate reference for you, express gratitude to the Universe or your Higher Power for all of the inspiration and courage that have been, is being and will be given to you.

6. On a scale of 1 to 10, with this project, how much do I really believe in my ability to make it happen successfully and why?

----

7. On a scale of 1 to 10, with this project, how much do I doubt my ability to make it happen successfully and why?

----

8. Write this affirmation by Henry Ford—"*Whether you believe you can do a thing or not, you are right.*"

    ----

9. How did you feel as you were writing the affirmation? What were you thinking ? How does this affirmation relate to you and your desire to make your dream a reality?

    ----

10. Describe a time when Inner Knowing led you to a new awareness about yourself and/or manifesting your vision.

    ----

8. Describe a time when you used appropriate action and achieved a victory because of it. How did you feel? What conclusions did you come to because of the outcome?

_____

_____

_____

_____

_____

_____

_____

Chapter 8

The number "8" is both a physical number *and* an ethereal number. It represents the actual physical manifestation of your original inspiration or idea. It's the number that shows the results of what you've committed your time, energy, efforts, willingness and resources to. It relates to success, stability, profit, time and synchronicity, as well as practicality and pragmatism. It also relates to limitations, belief systems, inflexibility, unwillingness and fear. It refers to the choices, both easy and hard, that must be made in order to edit or improve the physical manifestation of your vision.

At this stage, it all comes together and you see the actual results, the manifestation of your inspiration, your desire and your plans.

"Every great work, every big accomplishment, has been brought into manifestation through holding to the vision, and often just before the big achievement, comes apparent failure and discouragement."
–Florence Scovel Shinn

S tep 8 is the simplest and most challenging of all of the steps because it involves the balanced use of both physical and ethereal energies in order to bring a vision to physical completion.

Eight is the number and stage of mastery and classical duality. It's associated with Janus, the Roman god of gateways and time who, with his two faces, symbolizes the importance of acknowledging the past while being grounded in the present as we look forward to the future. The number '8' is also associated with the symbol for infinity, the lemniscate (the number '8' on its side = ∞). Upright, '8' represents the finite or material, physical plane; on its side, it represents the infinite, ethereal realm.

147

The theme of Step 8 in any endeavor is illustrated by these two phrases, *"It was the best of times, it was the worst of times"* and *"the agony and the ecstasy."*

All of these phrases, words, states of being and images will come into play as you work your way through this stage. With each descriptive word, phrase and character, the meaning of the number '8' becomes clearer as you're ushered through the gateway that leads to your success in achieving your vision.

1. *"It was the best of times, it was the worst of times."*

"It was the best of times, it was the worst of times." The opening sentence in one of Charles Dickens' greatest novels, *"A Tale of Two Cities,"* very aptly describes Step 8. The energy of this step can seem a tad schizophrenic at times because it operates in a two-fold manner.

On one hand there's the joy, exhilaration and sense of achievement that comes from knowing your vision has manifested into more than a hope, a wish or a concept, that all of your efforts weren't wasted and have come together as something that you can recognize and identify as the physical proof of your inspiration and ingenuity.

On the other hand, there's often doubt, a kind of emotional exhaustion and the disbelief that you can successfully, competently do the necessary work required to put the proper finishing touches on your project. The quote by Florence Scovill Shinn at the beginning of this chapter very fittingly illustrates my point—*"Every great work, every big accomplishment, has been brought into manifestation through holding to the vision, and often just before the big achievement, comes apparent failure and discouragement."*

2. *"The agony and the ecstasy of life, creation and being."*

In my experience, this seemingly schizophrenic stage is the most challenging of all of the other stages. Whenever you create, you're making something new, something that hasn't existed in this form before. You are literally working in a blind, learning how to physically make your creation as you're putting it together. The emotional impact is both thrilling and terrifying and you are never more alive as you wrestle with the various emotions and energies and try to convert them into something of physical substance and value, all the while trying to maintain the much needed perspective of objectivity and grace.

You must be willing to move through and beyond all you know, never really certain of whether or not your efforts will pay off, and continue working toward your goal, sometimes as if you were in the dark and could only know how to move and act by touch and hope and faith. Here, you must listen to the voice of your creation and let it direct you when all of your common sense tells you to take a short-cut or it's not worth all that you're putting into it. Or any of the million other things the mind will tell you in order to keep you from discovering a new, stronger, more courageous creator within yourself.

Here is where you will wrestle with all your limiting little demons, dragons and imps. And wrestle with them you will. On occasion, you'll lose a round and have to pick yourself up, dust yourself off and go back into the fray again and again and again until you finally best them. The good news is, it does get easier each time you create something new; the bad news is, some aspect of this 'agony' is always present in the realm of productive creativity. When I find myself in this place (and I do, every time), I've learned to remind myself that these thoughts and feelings always come up, especially at this stage of the process of creation. And I keep working at it, and eventually, I always come out the other side of this 'agony' into the 'ecstasy' of winning.

One of my dear friends is a very talented unknown artist. Beverly's unknown and likely to remain that way because she keeps trying to circumvent this part of the process of productive creativity. She has great ideas but rarely produces anything because she's unwilling to enter into and battle her way through this aspect of manifestation. The very wise sage and author, M. Scott Peck, writes that evil is a result of trying to avoid the pain of the hard, sometimes uncomfortable work that is required to discipline and transform yourself. I'd like to take that further and add that unappreciated genius and failed talent are often the result of trying to avoid the difficult and sometimes painful work of surrendering to the demands of intimate interaction with the creative process.

Beverly loves the first stages of creativity: the inspiration, ideas and desire phases. She hates the dealing with the unknown, the challenges and the obstacles phases. If she could enter into co-operative relationship with her creative spirit and produce her artwork without encountering any of the mundane and/or emotional challenges, pains and obstacles that typically accompany creative production, she would.

I don't blame her, so would I. However, it doesn't work like that. While Beverly strives to remain unscathed by any intimate interaction with her muse, her soul remains stunted and unsatisfied, her truth lies dormant and her life expression is rendered mute. And this can only lead to frustration, anger and the very real danger of becoming embittered.

Often, fear has a big presence in this step, *"Suppose I was wrong or I took a wrong turn and made a wrong decision somewhere along the way?"* *"Suppose no one likes what I create?"* *"Suppose..."* The list of supposes is as long as humankind's hopes and fears about catching lightning in a bottle—about creating and being a successful part of making magic and miracles. This step—8—is that part of the creative, manifesting process that so clearly describes our human journey toward creation and wholeness. This is another of those places where you want to just walk away from your project. Fear, doubt and/or realizing that all of your efforts have succeeded beyond your wildest expectations can trip you up if you let them.

In one of my many professional incarnations, I worked as a costumer and designer for television and films. Once, while working on a popular TV show, a hard-working, up and coming character actor was the guest star for that week's episode. The actor and everyone involved with the production knew that if he did well, the writers and producers were going to permanently hire him and write his character into the show.

There was a lot of buzz about it and the actor's agent and manager were there on the set with him. If this went well, they all knew that everyone's life was going to change. When I took the actor his wardrobe for his first scene, I could see that he was very tense and didn't seem confident at all. A certain amount of nervousness was to be expected, but his was way more intense than anything I'd seen before. When it came time to shoot the scene, he was so nervous that he kept blowing his lines. So much so, that a scene that should have taken half an hour to shoot, took four hours. And to make matters worse, he handled his inability to perform by becoming angry and verbally abusive to the crew.

Even though we all understood why he was acting out that way, it was still very hard to watch someone who'd worked so hard to get this opportunity, go down in flames. The scene was finally shot satisfactorily and the actor, having finished for the day, was sent home. The producers and writers had also been present on the set. Afterwards, they held an emergency meeting, re-wrote the episode, diminishing the actor's character to the two lines already shot and informed the actor's agent that for creative reasons, the episode would be going in a different direction and the actor's services would no longer be required on the show.

That actor had worked hard to get this big opportunity and had allowed the little demons, dragons and imps of anxiety, fear of change and self-doubt to sabotage himself. His fear was so palpable that we all knew he was subconsciously screwing up his lines and takes because he was afraid of the success that being on a hit show would bring him.

3. The number '8'

This is the place where you've gathered all of your projects components, materials and tools, as well as your experience, need and desire and must now bring all of them together so that they beautifully and profitably reflect what you're committed to. In this exciting and scary place, though, distractions abound and can falsely appear more appealing or beneficial to you. Sadly, this, too, is a place where many projects are abandoned because of these illusory distractions.

Step 8 is a gateway to the successful completion of your journey. It's also the long, often detail intense road to putting the proper finish on your project that will bring satisfaction to you and elicit appreciation from others when you present it to the world. In doing all the laborious and often monotonous tasks that it takes to complete or finish your project, your inspiration's new value and beauty begin to shine through and so does yours. Both of you are, in subtle and not so subtle ways, transformed. You and it become more than you were when you started. You become whole in some ethereal way just as your project becomes whole in the material realm. This "new birth" wouldn't have been possible if you hadn't begun and persevered on the journey you've taken to create something physical from the combined realms of the heart, mind and spirit.

This stage of the creative process is time consuming. Rarely the glamorous part of creating, this is the *"shoulder to the wheel, nose to the grindstone"* aspect and it demands parts of you that you didn't know existed and often makes those demands at times when you don't think you've got any more to give.

If you're an actor, this is where the director says, *"Great—now do it again—this time with more feeling,"* when you've just given the scene all the emotion you've got. And somehow, you've got to dig deeper to places you didn't know existed and find and project that depth of creative expression that the moment is calling for.

The finite and the infinite must come together. The only way to achieve that is to make your way through the dense maze of creative expression and productivity. Unlike many of my friends, the challenge of video games doesn't appeal to me, so I don't play them. Instead, I simply decide to create something. Once I've suited up and entered the density of whatever danger lurks in the creative maze in order to retrieve the prize most longed for, I encounter, do battle with and am sometimes nearly vanquished by the dragon of obstacles and opposition. Most of the time, I manage to emerge victorious with the prize in my hands and the knowing that by risking myself and all I knew, I've come out with more than I ever could have imagined. Because of the adventure, I've discovered some previously unknown part of myself and my soul, heart and I are thrilled in the most wonderful and wondrous ways.

Often the dragon looks like (and is) that laborious work I've mentioned before. Here, in addition to being the place where all of the different parts, pieces and elements come together, this is also the place where the finishing work must be done if your project is to have that beautiful, professional patina that will make it so attractive to your audience and to you. The actual physical structure, foundation and details that are key to the success of your project are refined here. The work and steps taken that are key to the success of your project but not obvious to the normal observer are performed in this step that often calls for late night (and in some cases, all night) completion sessions.

If you're a woodworker, this is the stage where the piece of furniture you've been building is ready for the step that will show off the beauty of your work and add to the value of the piece, as well as provide you with the satisfaction of seeing the physical result of your vision. In order for all of that to happen, though, you have to painstakingly sand the piece, meticulously wipe it down, carefully apply a thin coat of lacquer to it, patiently let the lacquer dry and when it does dry, start the process all over again, anywhere from ten to as many as thirty times to achieve the finish you want.

If your project manifests in the form of a business presentation, this is where you run countless errands to office supply and copy stores and spend hours putting your Power Point images together, making the sleek information folders to give to your audience and writing and practicing your sales pitch so that it appears to effortlessly, naturally roll off your tongue.

No matter what your project is, you're going to have to be that woodworker or that business presenter at this point. You're going to have to accept that you've arrived at the place where these unromantic, often repetitive and at times tedious tasks must be done and be done with as much gentleness, strength, commitment and courage as you can bring into consciousness.

What do I do to successfully get through this part? I look at the totality of the tasks ahead of me, acknowledge them and then purposely 'forget' all but the most immediate task as I begin to perform it, keeping in mind this affirmation, *"the best way to complete a difficult task is to complete the first step."* When I finish with that first step, the next task in line becomes the new 'first' step and I give it all of my attention. I do this until I've completed all of the 'polishing' tasks. It's a way of mentally taking a potentially overwhelming project and separating it into manageable bits.

And what do I tell myself when I want to quit? Practical, encouraging statements like, *"Each step I take now is one less step I have to take later,"* *"I'm going to win this, I'm not going to let this defeat me."* And when I'm really feeling up against it, I channel one of my favorite troubadours, Van Morrison, as I remember the name of one of his tours, *"Too late to turn back now."* Sometimes, I even print those statements out and put them up on the walls and mirrors of my home so that I'm constantly reminded and encouraged to *"keep on keepin' on."*

4. The lemniscate '∞', mastery, manifestation and immortality

The use of the word 'finish' is very important here. Used as a verb, *"she's finished the piece,"* it describes a work that is completed in all its details. Used as an adjective, *"the finishing application is all that's needed,"* it describes something used to perfect or complete a thing. Used as a noun, *"the finish on this piece really brings out the uniqueness of it,"* it describes the completed detailed surface or appearance of a thing.

Chapter 8 is written to give you strength and encouragement, as well as to acknowledge the importance and intensity of this step. This step is where the real transformation takes place. This is where the standing eight turns on its side and becomes the lemniscate symbolizing infinity and immortality. This is where your personal creative expression joins the Universal energy of creation and you and your vision become limitless, timeless, immortal. This is what greatness is: No matter how small or how large in the world your achievement is, it is a piece of the immortality of time and all existence. By manifesting it, you and it become a part of the limitlessness of all there is; you and your creation become infinite. This is the beauty and fun of a challenge, something wondrous and indescribable happens when we become involved in life in this way. Something so important, so intrinsic to the growth, development and evolution of the human spirit awakens and transports us to places our souls longed for but never knew existed until now. Here is where we discover the true prize—that we are more alive, vital and connected to the essence of life than ever before. And that's when we understand that the thing we were driven to create is not only our manifested vision, it's our trophy, our souvenir, the symbolic proof of our journey, there to remind us when we forget, that we are capable of making all of our dreams come true.

A few years ago, while visiting South America, I decided that as long as I was on the continent, it would be a good idea for me to visit Machu Picchu, Peru's wonderfully preserved Incan Empire city. Almost every aspect of my Peruvian experience was difficult, always testing and at times, almost besting me in some very intense manner. After finally getting to the site, finding my guide, channeling the previously illusive Spanish language so well that my guide was shocked that I was an American and navigating the slippery and somewhat dangerous natural stone steps, I found myself standing on a precipice, overlooking the preserved ruins of the ancient royal enclave and spiritual center.

From where I stood, my view matched the ones I'd seen in the photographs that had inspired me to make the trek up the mountain. Although the view was stunning, I didn't feel the same type of emotional-spiritual connection I usually feel at sacred sites. Thinking of all I'd gone through in order to be standing on that spot, I noted the lack of connection and silently wondered why I'd felt so compelled to be there. Just then, in answer to my question, these words went through my mind, "So *that you'd always know that your dreams can come true.*" The gift of that message was and continues to be priceless. It was the journey that was important, the view was my trophy, just as your completed project will be your trophy, the souvenir of a unique, life enhancing, transformative odyssey of creation, completion and satisfaction.

Work Book Exercises

"That which we persist in doing becomes easier, not that the task itself has become easier, but that our ability to perform it has improved."
—Ralph Waldo Emerson

1. Listen to *Stage 3– Steps 7 through 9* of the Guided Imagery meditation that comes with this book. Listening to this Guided Imagery meditation 15 minutes every day will help strengthen your determination and build your confidence as you continue the process of manifesting your vision. It will also help you connect your intuitive, creative, generating energy (feminine) to your intellectual, methodical, activating energy (masculine) which will heighten your level of magnetism and attract to you all manner of good luck, opportunities and helpful people and circumstances.

2. Before you go to bed, sit quietly for 15-20 minutes and listen to meditation music. Doing so will help you to more powerfully assimilate the experiences of your day and on an inner level, keep the center of creativity and desire—your heart chakra—open.

3. It's important to express gratitude. Expressing gratitude is more than just giving thanks. In addition to being an acknowledgement, it's also, to quote the author, Robert Emmons, *"a felt sense of wonder, thankfulness, and appreciation for life."* Gratitude places you in a state of grace and energetically positions you to be a magnet for the good you want to attract. Express gratitude to yourself for getting to this first stage of completion of your project. Express gratitude for the people, experiences, and blessings that have assisted you in getting to this point. And if it's an appropriate reference for you, express gratitude to the Universe or your Higher Power for all of the inspiration and courage that have been, is being and will be given to you.

4. Keep it simple. This step is the mundane, 'grunt' work that'll give your project the professional polish it needs and you'll need to fortify and encourage yourself with these 'helpers' and reminders.

5. Play music during this gathering and finishing phase. It doesn't matter what type of music, as long as it doesn't interfere with your process.

6. Print out and post encouraging affirmations in your work space. At the back of this book, you'll find a selection of affirmations to choose from or you can use encouraging affirmations from another source.

7. Remember to BREATHE. Breathing deeply, gently, rhythmically will keep your body energized and your brain activated.

8. Every hour or two, stop working and stretch your body or take a walk or dance to the music you're listening to. This kind of movement will dispel the physical and mental tension that happens as a result of such intense concentration.

9. Keep on keepin' on.

Chapter 9

The number "9" is a culmination number.
It represents the third stage of completion of any endeavor and is a time of personal acknowledgement and celebration. It relates to perfecting, packaging and presenting your project as well as re-determining its value. It refers to your emotional, mental and spiritual clarity and flexibility, as well as a need to rely on your inner strength as you complete your vision.

You have now reached the third stage of completion of your project. This chapter will clearly show you what and where you need to fine tune your project just before you take it out into the world (the marketplace).

"Great things are not done by impulse, but by a series of small things brought together."
—Vincent Van Gogh

Wow, you're almost done! You've gone through a lot to get here and now you can actually see and have in hand the tangible, physical manifestation of something that at one time, only existed in the ethereal realm as a hope, a wish or an idea.

This stage is the culmination stage, what I call the "salad bowl" stage. The combined results or "ingredients" of the previous eight steps, will tell you what kind of product or "salad" you've created as well as its value to yourself and the world. And, just as with any salad, here is where you get a chance to add or remove ingredients to tailor the "salad" to your particular taste.

It's at this stage that you test the results and fine-tune your vision or project and decide how and where it needs tweaking before it can be considered ready for the marketplace. Almost in its final form, your project just needs those finishing touches—drawer

158

pulls and handles for the woodworker's cabinet, buttons for the designer's coat, presentation folders for the entrepreneur's development pitch, flowers for that romantic proposal.

Nearly at the presentation point, polishing your project becomes an important issue as you apply the bells and whistles of fine-tuning and packaging that'll get your audience's attention and elicit their appreciation.

As you continue the fine tuning and the "test driving" of your now manifested vision, you can begin to congratulate yourself for the beauty you've created, the journey you've taken and the conscious realization of your infinite potential. Take delight in the knowledge that you're holding the proof that with commitment, desire and the right system, you CAN make the impossible possible and create the magic and miracles you want to have in your life!

Although there is still work to be done, it's important and it's good for you to acknowledge yourself and the results of your efforts as you enjoy this energetically satisfying "oasis" of well-deserved, self-congratulatory calm.

So, on with the finishing touches!

You may be standing in front of your creation, thinking, *"It's perfect, of course it'll do well and be received with open arms. I don't really need to test it."* Or maybe, you have personally tested it once or twice and deemed it "ready for prime time." Sometimes, that's all you need. Most of the time, though, you do need to test your completed vision in front of an objective audience, someone who, even if they love you, will play "devil's advocate" and ask tough questions, point out the flaws in your project and make positive, helpful suggestions that will make your manifested vision shine.

That kind of love is a very courageous kind. The person (or persons) who expresses it is risking the wrath of your ego if they notice that your manifested vision is less than your idea of perfect. Their priceless service to you is really a gift and their comments and suggestions are coming from a place of wanting you to succeed.

Ask your mentor or support group (or someone from a professional organization like S.C.O.R.E., the Service Corps of Retired Executives, an all-volunteer organization of mentors) to critique your project and give you suggestions that'll help you tweak it to perfection as you put the finishing touches on it. Remember, the opportunity to see your creation through other, more objective and experienced eyes, isn't always an easy opportunity for you to take, but it is always a richly rewarding one for you and your project.

You do have to be careful who you initially reveal your precious realized vision to, though. Counting on an honest, helpful appraisal from what I call the "toxic chorus," is a sure invitation to devaluing yourself and your project.

The "toxic chorus" is made up of people who are either jealous, afraid, lack vision or imagination, are destructively critical and/or pessimistic, or a combination of all of the above.

If they're jealous, they're going to be so threatened by your achieving something that makes you feel good about yourself that they'll do or say anything to make you feel like a loser.

If they're afraid, they're afraid of anything new, what people will think or say, that you will leave them if you're successful and/or that your accomplishment is living proof that their excuses for not living up to their full potential, are just that, excuses.

If they lack vision or imagination, they'll try to discourage you because they're trying to keep their beliefs narrow and their options limited. They've forgotten how to live in possibility and have hope. When dealing with them, just remember that old adage, "*Misery loves company.*"

And the most poisonous of all, those who are destructively critical and/or pessimistic. Destructively critical and/or pessimistic people live to throw water on your fire. If they can douse the spark or flame of creativity and joy in any person or situation, they're happy. For the most part, these people were raised in the same toxic atmosphere that they are now trying to infuse your life with. Their having been exposed to that type of abuse during their formative years is sad, but it's no excuse for them trying to inflict it on you.

All of these "toxic chorus" types will try to get you to believe they're helping you by protecting you from pain and disappointment. Please don't buy into that. They don't want you to see who they really are and what they're really doing. Protect your dream and the dreamer, you, from the corrosive, dream killing effects of these emotional vampires. And like all things toxic, stay away from them.

"But what if the "toxic chorus" is comprised of my family or my friends or my spouse?" Yes, that's a tough one. When your emotional inner circle is coming from a place that only reflects their allegiance to what makes them feel safe and comfortable (even if it's gnarly), instead of coming from a genuinely heart-centered place where, despite their fears, they want you to succeed, you'll often feel torn or feel like you're betraying them in some way by honoring your heart and following your own path. This is another great reason to find a mentor who isn't a member of the family or your peer group. You will have to make sure that you have chosen a very strong support system to counteract the emotional tug-of-war you're likely to experience.

With the assistance of your strong determination, mentoring groups like S.C.O.R.E., your affirmations and a fantastic role model, someone who succeeded despite heavy opposition, you'll move through and beyond the emotional traps that that kind of environment can set for any visionary.

If you come from a different, more supportive environment and you've been careful about who you've chosen as your support team, you'll have a completely different experience. They'll value you and your vision and they'll be happy for you and want you to succeed as they encourage you in every possible way. Even those times when you decide that some portion of their advice isn't right for you, you'll still know what it's like to be acknowledged, valued and respected.

Hopefully, on this quest, you've made an ally of the indispensable quality of discernment, the ability to have keen insight and use good judgment, as you work your way through the detail-rich finishing steps of completing your project. In marketing, packaging and display are as important as the actual item being sold. Even if you disagree with those in your support system about some of the final details, be willing to be objective and see the big picture from their perspective.

When Marco moved to a town on the coast after working as a sous chef in restaurants in New York and Paris, he brought with him the desire to make one of his long held dreams a concrete reality, owning an Italian-American-Senegalese fusion restaurant. His desire to create a unique dining experience using ingredients and dishes from these three world regions stemmed from his unique perspective of having been born in Italy, trained at an American culinary school and raised by parents who were from the African nation of Senegal.

After successfully following steps 1 through 8, he arrived at Step 9 where he was advised to have a series of "soft openings" before he invited the region's top travel agencies, city guide organizations and travel publications to a complimentary evening at his new establishment.

Although he knew the importance of and had been advised to hold a "soft opening," he was unwilling to follow that advice because he was impatient. Marco's impatience and unwillingness to "wait productively" almost cost him his dream.

(A restaurant "soft opening" takes place just before a restaurant officially opens for regular business. Not yet open to the public, the owners and staff invite close friends and family to experience the food, service and ambiance and give honest appraisals of their experience. It's a great way to smooth out any rough spots, begin interacting with diners and gauge the public's likely reactions to the new establishment.)

A restaurant's soft opening, an out-of-town debut for a Broadway show and a rehearsal all serve the same purpose. They give you a real time experience in presenting your production to the world so that you can actually see what works and what doesn't in front of an audience. And just as importantly, you get to adjust and change what needs to be dealt with in order to make your presentation a hit before you present it to your target audience.

Marco meticulously planned his restaurant's opening. He was confident that, because he'd worked in restaurants for years, he'd be able to easily handle whatever problems arose during the course of the opening. As it turned out, Marco's misplaced confidence almost cost him his reputation, his business and the goodwill of the locals in his neighborhood.

Marco hadn't counted on the dearth of legal parking spaces in his area. The frustrations that ensued for many of his prospective business contacts (used to valet parking), meant that by the time they reached the restaurant, many of them were in a bad mood. He'd also miscalculated the amount of time needed for each dining group's seating, so those with later reservations had to wait outside of the restaurant because his small bar area was already overcrowded with delayed diners still waiting to be seated. Those frustrated, hungry people, forced to wait outside, blocked the narrow sidewalk and loudly complained to each other and passers-by about the way they were being treated. Many of the perspective diners left before they could be served, vowing to tell everyone about their unsatisfying experience at Marco's new restaurant.

Marco's neighbors weren't happy with him either. Aside from having to deal with the unhappy overflow in front of the new establishment and the diner's cars illegally blocking their driveways and parking lots, Marco hadn't followed the local custom of inviting the owners of the neighboring businesses to a pre-opening wine and hors d'oeuvres tasting.

Although, miraculously having no problems with the food or the service on his opening night, Marco's restaurant opening was a failure. Once the word got out about the inconveniences and frustrations of attempting to dine at his place, his hoped for endorsements from the travel industry would never come through.

Humbled, Marco was finally ready to listen to his advisors. After a night of brain-storming, they came up with a plan to salvage whatever goodwill they could from the disgruntled would-be diners and his insulted neighbors. Fortunately for him, he had very loyal investors, employees and friends who helped him implement the salvage plan.

The next morning, before too many damaging phone calls could be made by the unhappy (and presumably still hungry) unserved diners, each of them received a visit from one of Marco's support team. Each team member, in their own way, delivered a large bouquet of flowers, an eloquent apology and an invitation to dine at the restaurant along with a chauffeur driven limousine to take them there and drive them home afterwards. Since many of Marco's staff were also in show business, the apologies were unique, entertaining and memorable. The most talked about and envied apology was delivered by a waitress, skilled at prestidigitation, who mimed the heartfelt elaborate delivery of the apology along with an imaginary bouquet of flowers that turned into an actual bouquet of red roses, sunflowers and stargazer lilies.

Almost every one of the apology-invitations was accepted. And each guest's willingness to trust Marco's new promise was rewarded with a memorably delicious dining experience accompanied by a seemingly endless flow of champagne. Marco's great "save" attempt worked and enabled him to have a very profitable relationship with the travel agencies and their related businesses, thus ensuring his creative and financial successes.

While Marco's support team was delivering apologies to the travel industry professionals, he visited each of the businesses in his neighborhood, apologized to the owners for his ignorance in not honoring their custom and invited each of them and their families to a night of dining and entertainment. They happily accepted and at the conclusion of their meal, they embraced him and welcomed him to the neighborhood.

Marco's cautionary tale ends happily. He was lucky; it could have gone the other way for him. His impatience and unwillingness to see beyond his emotional myopic range caused him to make some huge mistakes. By not listening to his advisors and choosing not to have a soft opening before he invited people important to the success of his restaurant to dine there, he could have lost all he'd worked for. His refusal to get the value of and honor the neighborhood customs was a near fatal mistake, as well. If he'd used discernment and followed the advice of his support team, he'd have saved himself time, money and goodwill and he'd never have put his dream in jeopardy.

Whatever your project is, give yourself and it the gift of rehearsing your presentation before you unveil it to your intended audience. No matter what form your "soft opening" must take, it's worth it to expose and iron out the kinks so that you and your presentation will have a smooth, effortless, natural flow. Remember, powerfully presented is powerfully received.

If your project is a business proposal, practice making your presentation with all of the props, handouts and media equipment you'll use in the actual presentation. It's especially important to make sure the media equipment and the props are easy to operate and handle. Try not to have an *"oops, that isn't the right slide"* moment happen. If you've ever witnessed one of those, you know how much it can interrupt the flow and cause the audience's attention to drift away from you and your presentation. Practice your timing! Keep it concise, upbeat, informative and interesting. We've all been to those presentations that seemed to just go on and on and on until we eventually lost interest and zoned out. If you're using hand-outs, make a few extra copies. It's better to have some left over at the end of your presentation than too few to hand out during your presentation.

Any project that involves a presentation to other people will benefit from your practicing your presentation in front of a mirror and then in front of a group of supportive, positive people who will give you honest, helpful feedback. If you can, video your presentation. If you don't have a support group or access to a video camera, practice your presentation in front of a mirror. You'll get comfortable with it and you and your presentation will "bond" with each other, ensuring that effortless flow that'll guarantee you rapt attention and a successful presentation.

If your project is one that doesn't need an actual presentation in front of a gathered audience, it still needs its own type of "soft opening." When I finish making one of my coats, I put it on and go for a walk around my neighborhood or wear it to the grocery store. I ask myself these questions, *"Does it keep me warm?" "Is it comfortable to wear?" "Are the sleeves too tight?" "How does it hang on my body?"* I take the information I get from that test run and make whatever changes are necessary to make sure the coat and I work well together. After I've made those changes, I take it for another test run to make sure I've made all of the corrections I need to make. I repeat this step until I'm satisfied that my coat is what I want and need it to be.

Sometimes, your "soft opening" experience can come in an unexpected way. A few years ago, I bought a pair of old chairs from a friend. They were dark, heavy, masculine pieces of furniture in bad shape, but I could see something in them that no one else could. I stripped them of their dark paint, created a unique pale gold iridescent paint color and finish for them, replaced the spires with small quartz crystal balls and upholstered the seats and arms in a fabric that seemed to have been woven especially for them. I was a day away from making the pillows that would cover and cushion the backs of the chairs when another friend dropped by for a visit. Although she hadn't seen the chairs in their original state, she loved what I'd done to them. She strongly discouraged me from covering the backs as I'd intended, pointing out that the wave design of the back slats more than made up for any discomfort I was afraid I might experience without the padding of a cushion. She has impeccable taste and a great sense of style, so I really listened to what she had to say. Because I was willing to hear her critique, I took the risk and deviated from my original plan and I eliminated the back cushions. I'm so glad I did! The wave pattern of the back slats accentuated the beauty, grace and grandeur of what had become my elegant new throne chairs. Every time I look at them and comfortably sit back in them, I thank my dear friend, Delores, for her keen eye and fabulous taste.

Step 9 is so important! I can't stress the points in this chapter enough. You're almost at the finish line. Follow the advice in this step and you'll guarantee yourself a big win!

Work Book Exercises

"To finish first you must first finish."—Rick Mears

1. Listen to *Stage 3– Steps 7 through 9* of the Guided Imagery meditation that comes with this book. Listening to this Guided Imagery meditation 15 minutes every day will help strengthen your determination and build your confidence as you continue the process of manifesting your vision. It will also help you connect your intuitive, creative, generating energy (feminine) to your intellectual, methodical, activating energy (masculine) which will heighten your level of magnetism and attract to you all manner of good luck, opportunities and helpful people and circumstances.

2. Before you go to bed, sit quietly for 15-20 minutes and listen to meditation music. Doing so will help you to more powerfully assimilate the experiences of your day and on an inner level, keep the center of creativity and desire—your heart chakra—open.

3. It's important to express gratitude. Expressing gratitude is more than just giving thanks. In addition to being an acknowledgement, it's also, to quote the author, Robert Emmons, *"a felt sense of wonder, thankfulness, and appreciation for life."* Gratitude places you in a state of grace and energetically positions you to be a magnet for the good you want to attract. Express gratitude to yourself for getting to this third stage of completion of manifesting your vision. Express gratitude for all of the assistance you've been given in getting to this point. And if it's an appropriate reference for you, express gratitude to the Universe or your Higher Power for all of the inspiration, courage and good fortune that continue to accompany you on your journey.

4. If your project is a presentation, practice it at least three times before you present it to your target audience. (You can practice it more than three times but you don't want to practice it so much that you take the feeling of naturalness and vibrancy away

from it.) If you can, practice it in front of your mentor or someone from your support group. Get comfortable working with your media equipment and your hand-outs and make whatever final adjustments are called for.

5. If a formal or group presentation isn't necessary to the success of your project, it still needs you to test it out and make sure it works smoothly. Invite a friend over to review your handy-work; if it's feasible, take the results of your efforts out into the world as I do with my coats. Make whatever final adjustments are necessary.

6. Take some time to acknowledge yourself for how far you've come, for how much you've learned and for how powerful you've become.

Chapter 10

The number "10" is a completion or fulfillment number.
It represents the final stage of completion of any endeavor—the finished product, result or pay-off of any enterprise. It relates to the completion of one phase, which opens the way for the beginning of another phase and is the marker by which you can gauge the growth and success of yourself and your endeavor on the spiritual, emotional, creative and physical levels. It refers to the completed, valued result of the union of your generating self and your activating self, as well as the result of your union with those who helped you achieve your goal.

You have now reached the final stage of completion of your project. This chapter will show you how to recognize and appreciate yourself and all of your efforts and the results of those efforts, whether your project turned out as you initially envisioned it or not.

"It's kind of fun to do the impossible."
—Walt Disney

"I have the simplest tastes. I am always satisfied with the best."
—Oscar Wilde

I t's a wrap!" Your successfully completed project is and will be rewarding in more ways than you are aware of. Know that all that you've done to arrive at this point of the final stage of completion has added to and enriched you and the value of your life's journey. This achievement and all of the one's to follow, will profitably add to the establishment and continued building of your personal legacy and dynasty. Know too, that in this, as in all areas of life, the fine-tuning process will continue to generate newer and better ideas for the manifestation of all of your future hopes, wishes and ideas.

As you look at your completed project, know that it is actual proof that you can create magic and perform miracles. What was once only a wish, a hope or a dream is now a viable entity in your world, something real that exists in form where just a while ago, it was only an amorphous idea.

And as you look at yourself, know that the most important thing of all has happened: YOU have been transformed, too. In initiating and completing the manifestation of your vision, you have successfully completed your own version of Odysseus' journey home, complete with all of the monsters, temptations and illusions that interjected themselves and interfered with his progress. On this journey to fulfillment, you have also experienced and encountered your own version of all of the magical, miraculous, previously unforeseen help and occurrences that revealed themselves to you and assisted and accompanied you on this journey of creation, manifestation, self-discovery and self-mastery.

What can you expect from others in the world when you present your manifested vision to them? What will they say? How will they respond to your interpretation of manifested creation?

I have the answer to all three of those questions and it's the same answer for each of them—*"I don't know."*

How people will respond or react to anything, especially if it's new, is always, on some level, a mystery. Ask any comedienne who has practiced and perfected a comedic bit in front of countless audiences until she knows how and at what point during the bit that the laughs will come. She knows this particular bit will always work, and it always does—until she gets in front of an audience who, for some unknown reason, unlike all of the other audiences she's performed in front of, don't get the joke. As disappointing as that must be, she knows that her material is good and if she has to make some changes to her act to make it work, as long as the changes don't intrude on the integrity of her act, she makes those changes.

In actuality, it's rare that you won't have to make changes once you present your project to your target audience. That's a normal occurrence, even with all of the previous fine tuning. Sometimes, your awareness that changes are needed comes from an outside perspective and sometimes, that awareness comes from you. Whatever the source, if you agree that even after your presentation, the changes will make your project better—make the changes.

Life is organic. It's constantly changing and we are continually evolving and so are our ideas, visions, and creations. By listening with your heart and experiencing in real time the evolution of your vision, your creation will always be reflective of you and you and it will always be relevant to the present in some way.

When I made my latest coat, a magnificent homage to the era of the Medici's and the splendor of Versailles, I wore it to Florence, Italy, where the coat and I were received like royalty. Where ever I wore the coat, people who were used to seeing the grandest of creations, stopped what they were doing, exclaimed their admiration for its beauty and just had to touch it and talk to me about it. My favorite compliment came the last night I was there. I was in a supermarket, when behind me, I heard a woman yelling something in Italian. I turned around and there she was, an old woman in her seventies, excitedly pointing at me and screaming "*La vostra cappotto è bella!*" Not really sure what she was saying, I pointed to my coat and, in Italian, asked, "*This coat?*" She responded, "*Si, bellissima! Bellisima!*"

That moment was worth everything I'd gone through in order to make the coat (and I went through a lot). It was sweet. I loved it and I am and will be forever grateful for it because it added to the beauty of the inspirational, adventurous, liberating journey I took in making the garment. I knew (and continue to know) that from my soul's vision, like a butterfly, I was magnificently transformed as I manifested one of the finest garments ever made and it was lovely to have someone see and get my creative soul's intentions.

In writing this book, I've walked through every one of the steps that brought me here to Step 10. Sometimes, I was completely on board and supportive of myself as I wrote and sometimes I was totally resistant to trusting that I was doing the right thing. At times, I felt as though I was walking through fire as I questioned my ability and my right to express myself. I'm fortunate in that I have an amazing capacity for tenacity and that I have been blessed with a fantastic support team who believe in me and value my creations and won't allow me to rest on my laurels. I'm so grateful that they expect more of me because they know I have so much more to give and receive.

And that is what I know about you, as well. You have so much more to give and receive, too. You are a person of infinite possibilities. Do yourself and the rest of us a favor and let your creative light shine and manifest your dreams as it leads you to the life of happiness, satisfaction and richness your heart craves and you deserve.

There's a story in Hollywood, that several years ago, when a Grammy award winning singer, was about to go into the studio to record his first album, he told his friend, a legendary performer and music producer, that he didn't know if he was up to singing well enough to make the album. His friend put his hand on the singer's shoulder, looked him in the eyes and told him, *"That's OK, man, just go into that studio and do what you do and do it good."* And that's what the award winning singer did—every time he recorded a song.

So when you're doubting yourself or feeling in any way inadequate, just picture me, standing there with my hand on your shoulder, looking you in the eyes and reciting this great success mantra— ***"Do what you do and do it good."***

And now—without further ado—it's time to take a deep breath, unveil your project, present it to the world and take a much deserved bow.

Work Book Exercises

"Make a joyful noise!" —Psalm 100

"Among the mind's powers is one that comes of itself to many children and artists. It need not be lost, to the end of his days, by anyone who has ever had it. This is the power of taking delight in a thing, or rather in anything, not as a means to some other end, but just because it is what it is."

—Charles E. Montague

1. Admire your work and listen to *Stage 4– Step 10* of the Guided Imagery meditations that come with this book. Listening to this Guided Imagery meditation 15 minutes every day that you're putting the finishing touches on your project will help strengthen your determination and build your confidence as you come to the completion of manifesting your vision. It will also help you connect your intuitive, creative, generating energy (feminine) to your intellectual, methodical, activating energy (masculine) which will heighten your level of magnetism and attract to you all manner of good luck, opportunities and helpful people and circumstances.

2. Before you go to bed, sit quietly for 15-20 minutes and listen to meditation music. Doing so will help you to more powerfully assimilate the experiences of your day and on an inner level, keep the center of creativity and desire—your heart chakra— open.

3. It's important to express gratitude for your journey and for arriving at this point in the manifestation of your vision. Expressing gratitude is more than just giving thanks. In addition to being an acknowledgement, it's also, to quote the author, Robert Emmons, *"a felt sense of wonder, thankfulness, and appreciation for life."* Gratitude places you in a state of grace and energetically positions you to be a magnet for the good you want to attract. Express gratitude to yourself for getting to this final stage of completion of creating your vision. Express gratitude for all of the assistance you've been given in getting to

173

this point. And if it's an appropriate reference for you, express gratitude to the Universe or your Higher Power for all of the inspiration, courage, protection and blessings that continue to come your way.

4. **Celebrate and honor the do-er—YOU!** Treat yourself to something nice, you deserve it. And while you're drinking that glass of Champagne (or juice, soda or whatever you fancy), look at and/or think about your creation brought to life by you and congratulate yourself on being the victorious being of Light, creativity, magic and power that you are.

5. Now that you've completed your quest, what changes have you noticed in yourself?

----

6. What changes have you noticed in the people around you?

----

7. How do you feel about yourself now and your experience of creating what you wanted?

Appendix

"What if I don't know what I want?"

"Dream lofty dreams, and as you dream, so you shall become. Your vision is the promise of what you shall one day be; your ideal is the prophecy of what you shall at last unveil."
—James Allen

On some level, we all know what we want. Sometimes, we just need a little help identifying it. If you don't think you know what you want, the "Hmm Journal," is a perfect exercise and tool for helping you discover and clearly identify what you want. The "Hmm Journal" is a written record of those meaningful moments when your heart acknowledges what's important to you.

The "Hmm Journal" gets its name from the spontaneous sound we make when we see or think of something or someone that intuitively piques our interest in a very personal way and has us consciously or unconsciously considering its value to us. It's a soft melodious sound that feels like it comes from the heart as it gently vibrates the vocal chords.

It differs from the expressions, "*Oh!*" or "*Aha!*" because those sounds indicate a conscious evaluation process or arrived at conclusion in the determination of something or someone's value to us. They have a sharp or hard sound that seems to originate in our minds.

It's the things we say, "*hmm,*" about that tell us what we're truly interested in. Those are the things that speak to our souls in some way and remind us of what is genuinely meaningful to us on an inner level.

To create your own "Hmm Journal," you'll need a book with blank pages, (it doesn't have to be expensive; a notebook from your local office supply or discount store will do), and a pen. Keep the book, your "Hmm Journal," and pen with you at all times.

Whenever you see someone doing an interesting job, write the job title in your "Hmm Journal," It doesn't have to be a job you personally want to do, it just has to pique your interest and appeal to you in some personal way.

Here are three examples of some of my *"hmm"* experiences:

When I moved to New England, I noticed that a police officer was assigned to road works projects for traffic control. This was during the summer and I thought about how wonderful it was that the officer was outside and able to relax and be sociable as he made a contribution to society. It was such a lovely scene that I automatically found myself saying, *"hmm."* Now, I don't want to be a police officer or work on a road crew. And I definitely don't envy them when the weather is bad. But that day, when I drove past the road crew, I saw someone who was in charge of his day and time, who was enjoying his companions and surroundings, who was performing an important function and who was being paid to be there. That's what appealed to me and made me go, *"hmm."*

Another example are my two favorite TV hosts, the inimitable Oprah Winfrey and the Travel Channel's delightful Samantha Brown.

I am delighted that Oprah and I are on the planet at the same time. Every time I see her, I'm moved by her graceful vulnerability, personal courage, genuine, down-to-earth quality and fabulous sense of style as she lives her life out loud while using the power of her influence to transform her life and ours. She has a generosity of spirit that includes the whole world as she encourages others to discover and celebrate the brilliance of their own essence. Rather than pander to lowered expectations, she takes risks and continues to embrace the infinite potential of life. Like a best friend, she encourages all of us by her presence and her example to do the same.

I watch Samantha Brown's travel shows as much for her as I do the places she visits. Like Oprah, she exudes a down-to-earth genuineness that leaves you feeling like a friend. In order to fulfill her function as host of her show, she has to travel to some of the most interesting places in the world, be granted special access to the most beautiful sites and artwork in existence, meet and mingle with fascinating people from all walks of life and have the most unique and exciting experiences ever, all the while getting paid! What's not to like about that!?

Needless to say, these two women elicit a great big *"hmm,"* from me. I get the feeling that their hosting jobs are just vehicles for them to get our attention so that they can demonstrate the Divine intention for all of us, to joyfully live life to the fullest.

My third example of *"hmm"* elicitation comes from a trip to one of my favorite cities, Paris. (I love Leonardo Da Vinci's painting of the Mona Lisa so much that once, I went to Paris just to visit her at the Louvre.) On this particular trip, I encountered Madame Laurent, Mona Lisa's guard at the Louvre. Her job is to stand in front of the web belt barrier about twelve feet from the famed painting and keep the ever present crowd from getting too close to it. Between Mona Lisa and the web belt barrier stands a curved wooden railing about five feet from the painting.

I was able to stand right at center front of the web belt barrier, so I had an unobstructed view of the woman that legendary singer, Nat "King" Cole, describes in his song as *"the lady with the mystic smile."* Keeping the adoring fans from pushing past the barrier and getting too close, was the very efficient, stern, uniformed guard, whose name tag read, *"Laurent."* As she perused the crowd, she kept order and wasn't hesitant at all to sharply caution us to stay behind the web belt barrier, something she had to do often because we just wanted to be near Mona.

Wishing I could get closer, I adoringly basked in the presence of my beloved Mona, when I noticed that every once in a while, the stern Madame Laurent would spot a child in the crowd. Her face would soften and with a look of loving kindness in her eyes, she would beckon the child forward, lift the web barrier and direct the child to stand at the curved wooden railing. As I watched in fascination, I saw her do this at least a dozen times, to the delight of the little chosen ones. I was moved at how fortunate those children were; at how much the stern guard loved Mona and knew the value of the priceless gift of the heart that she gave the children by bringing them so close to this legendary symbol of beauty, mystery and grace that we all connect with no matter what our age or background. In addition to being fascinated by Madame Laurent's acts of generosity and grace, I noticed that each time she let one of the children stand closer to Mona, for two or three seconds, she had to struggle to arrange her face back into a stern mask as she turned to face the crowd again.

The delighted look on the children's faces as they stood at the curved wooden railing and gazed at Mona was all the confirmation anyone needed that Madame Laurent was doing Divine work. My heart was as filled with wonder and beauty at this display of selfless generosity as it was by being in the presence of the Mona Lisa. I knew that I wanted to connect with Madame Laurent and share with her what she had given me that day, and I wanted to do it in French, the language of the heart. (Which was going to be interesting because my command of the French language is practically nil and I'm intimidated at the prospect of mangling such a beautiful language in my attempts to communicate. When I do speak it, even the most adamant proponent of the language will say to me, *"That's very nice that you tried—we will speak English now."*)

As I prepared myself to leave that place of infinite love and beauty, I managed to put into words—in French, no less!—what was in my heart. I approached her and when she turned to me, I looked into her eyes and in the best French I could muster, told her, *"Madame Laurent, I have seen with my heart, the beauty and the grace of your heart, and I am grateful. Thank you."*

We looked into each other's eyes and saw the reflections of our own hearts, which we knew in that moment, to be the reflection of the Divine's heart. She smiled and nodded at the acknowledgement and I turned to leave as she turned back to her work.

So, where's the *"hmm"* in that experience? The seemingly stern guard, Madame Laurent, spent a good portion of her day in an environment filled with priceless works of incomparable beauty, in charge of the experience of one of the most beloved art treasures of the world, with the power and the desire to share that experience in such a way that we, the recipients of this gift, were able to connect with the Divine in ourselves and be transformed by it—all the while getting paid _and_ living in Paris!

You get the idea of what a *"hmm"* experience is now, don't you? It's an experience that resonates with you as it inspires you to expand your idea of that wonderful phenomenon called possibility.

How To Use Your "Hmm Journal":

Carry it with you at all times for twenty-one (21) days. Whenever you see, hear, read or think about a profession that causes you to go, *"hmm,"* jot the job title down in your "Hmm Journal."

Based on my examples, my "Hmm Journal" would look like this:

1- Police officer on a beautiful summer day works with a road crew

2- Oprah and Samantha Brown host their shows

3- Madame Laurent guards Mona Lisa and touches our hearts

Do this for the three-week (21 days) duration of the exercise. (The mind takes 21 days to create a new habit and adjust to change.)

You'll discover that what's happening for you is this: you're beginning to think and live in the state of possibility. Your sense of adventure and discovery are being awakened, your imagination is being stimulated and you're consciously connecting to what is in your heart. There is a sense of limitlessness, freedom and power that comes with embracing possibility. You'll feel it in every fiber of your being and you'll see it in everything you think of.

After three weeks (21 days), take a look at the job descriptions you've jotted down in your "Hmm Journal." Even if they're wildly different occupations, you'll begin to notice that many of them share similar qualities, and that's what you're looking for—the qualities that appeal to you and motivate you.

Make a list of the qualities and put the journal away for 24 hours. At the end of the 24 hours, read your list of qualities and you'll notice that you've begun to be able to think of ideas that you want to actualize. Write those ideas down and don't censor yourself! As you write, one idea will stand out more than the others; that's the one you want to begin to manifest.

A note of caution, however: beware of buyer's remorse! Buyer's remorse often crops up when a person makes a decision about something and begins to commit to it. Simply put, it's a *"grass is greener"* or *"I know I chose this thing, but now, the other thing looks better"* idea that 99% of the time is only an illusion. Whatever you choose, when buyer's remorse enters the picture, the other option almost always looks like the better choice; it's human nature. You can avoid sinking into confusion and wasting a lot of time and energy by sticking with your first choice.

If you just can't let yourself do that or there are two or three options that seem to be calling out to you, there is a solution. Get as many small pieces of paper as you have options (if you have more than three options, you don't have buyer's remorse, you're being indecisive and you need to be 'no nonsense' about the process of choosing and eliminate all but three of your options). Write one option down per each piece of paper and fold each of those pieces of paper into a small square. Put the folded pieces of paper into a hat or a bowl. Close your eyes, swish the folded pieces of paper around in the hat or bowl, put your hand into the hat or bowl and pick <u>one</u> of the pieces of paper. The option you choose <u>is</u> the correct option for you at this time. And yes, the other options you didn't choose will start to look better than the one you did choose, but they aren't. All that remains for you to do now is commit to the option you chose and get started on manifesting your vision by re-reading Chapter 1 and doing the work book exercise at the end of the chapter.

Role Models

"For we have not even to risk the adventure alone, for the heroes of all time have gone before us..."
—Joseph Campbell

A role model is someone whom you admire and who inspires you because of their accomplishments. Role models are helpful to us because they symbolize that someone, a human being just like you, can triumph over adversity and achieve their goals.

When we admire something about someone, we're admiring a value, quality or trait that is also in us. Especially in the case of a role model, the person will reflect the value, quality or trait you have that you need to strengthen and develop within yourself.

The best way to choose a role model is to look back through history and choose someone whose contributions to society and whose accomplishments and journey through life inspire you. Although family members and current popular celebrities can be obvious and tempting choices for role models, it's best if you don't choose them. There is often too much emotion or drama around them that prevents you from having an objective perception of them and their impact on your world.

Once you've chosen your role model, read everything you can find about them and remember, you're also learning about a very important and powerful aspect of yourself, too. If possible, find a photograph or painting of them and put it where you can see it every day. If you can't find a likeness of them, write their name on a piece of paper, put it in a picture frame and put it where you can see it every day. You'll find a list of possible role models at the end of this chapter.

As you go about making your vision a physical reality, you'll find that the essence or spirit of your role model's great qualities bring out, emphasize and support the power of your talents, abilities and perseverance.

Your role model will also serve to encourage you when you begin to doubt yourself, especially when well-meaning friends, relatives and so-called experts insist that you're just kidding yourself and wasting your time by working to make your dream a physical reality.

I have different role models for the different aspects of my life and professions. The ones who are always constants in my life, though, are Harriet Tubman, a former slave in the pre-civil war South whose dignity and freedom were so important to her that she not only escaped her inhumane forced servitude, she courageously and successfully, repeatedly risked her own life to go back into the South to lead other slaves to freedom; Miss Piggy (I know, I know, she's not a real person but some of her life philosophies are so right on!), a muppet who espouses some salient truths we could all learn from, like, *"There is no one on the planet to compare with moi,"* and Helen Keller, an author, activist and lecturer who, though deaf and blind since childhood, chose not to suffer from her limitations, but to thrive and live meaningfully despite them. In so doing, she overcame those disabilities and limitations and went on to live a full life and accomplish many great things. Her positive perspective on life is a great inspiration to me.

As you can see, there are many different sources from which I draw inspiration. Role models are living proof that *"life is what you make it."* If you can't think of a role model, go on line and research the people on this list of possible candidates for you to choose from. In doing your research, you may come across someone who appeals to you who isn't on this list. If so, great! If they resonate with you, go with it.

List of Inspirational Role Models

Mahatma Gandhi
Dr. Martin Luther King, Jr.
Eleanor Roosevelt
Golda Meir
Leonardo Da Vinci
Mark Twain
Ludwig Van Beethoven
Frederick Douglass

Andrew Carnegie
Mary Kay Ash
Thomas Edison
Albert Einstein
Ralph Waldo Emerson
Henry David Thoreau
Dr. Charles Drew
Sir Edmund Hillary
Vince Lombardi
Rosa Parks
Amelia Earhart
Jackie Robinson
Princess Diana
Ida B. Wells
Aung Sang Suu Kyi
Nelson Mandela
Dalai Lama
Louise Hay
Muhammad Ali
Oprah Winfrey
Buck Brannaman
Bree Newsome

"That some achieve great success, is proof to all that others can achieve it as well."

— Abraham Lincoln

Affirmations

The importance of affirmations and other encouraging words is legendary. Affirmations are just that—they help us affirm that we are not alone in our quest for greatness. They serve to remind us that, at times, we all need to know that we are being guided and supported. Dr. Mardy Grothe put it best when he said, "*At every stage of my life, well-phrased aphorisms from a wide assortment of writers have stimulated my thinking, challenged my preconceptions, provided new perspectives on challenges I was facing, helped me find my way when I was lost, and in general inspired me to become a better person.*"

Let these affirmations accompany and guide you as you seek and find your greatness. Choose the ones that encourage and resonate with you. Print them out and put them on the inside of your entry doors, at the top of your mirrors, on your refrigerator door, on the dashboard of your car. These are all places that we look at and are aware of on conscious and unconscious levels. By putting your affirmations in these places, the power of their energy will effortlessly work to bring inspiration and confidence to you.

"The big question is whether you are going to be able to say a hearty 'yes' to your adventure."
—Joseph Campbell

"This is the purpose of life—to get what you want. There are deeper things, but this is fun."
—Karl Lagerfeld

"Creativity represents a miraculous coming together of the uninhibited energy of the child combined with the sense of order imposed on the disciplined adult intelligence."
—Norman Podhoretz

"Make a joyful noise!"
—Psalm 100

"You're special and unique among all the creatures on the planet earth. You've been endowed with the capacity and the power to create desirable pictures inside your mind and to find them automatically printed in the outer world of your environment. All your dreams can come true, if you have the courage to pursue them."

—The Daily Guru

"Success is not a secret; it is a system."

—Florence Scovel Shinn

"Among the mind's powers is one that comes of itself to many children and artists. It need not be lost, to the end of his days, by anyone who has ever had it. This is the power of taking delight in a thing, or rather in anything, not as a means to some other end, but just because it is what it is."

—Charles E. Montague "

Happiness lies in the joy of achievement and the thrill of creative effort."

—Franklin D. Roosevelt

"True happiness comes from the joy of deeds well done, the zest of creating things new."

—Antoine de Saint-Exupery

"Some pursue happiness—others create it."

—Unknown

"The secret of happiness is freedom. The secret of freedom is courage."

—Thucydides

"Happiness is when what you think, what you say, and what you do are in harmony."

—Mahatma Gandhi

"The greatest happiness is to transform one's feelings into action."

—Madame de Stael

186

"Fear is energy. Energy is innocent; it's what I do with it that determines the outcome."

—Reverend Aldridge

"You may be disappointed if you fail, but you will be doomed if you do not try."

—Unknown

"God's delays are not necessarily God's denials."

—Errol Van Mannen

"You are free to believe what you choose and what you do attests to what you believe."

—A Course of Miracles

"Don't let the noise of other people's opinions drown out your inner voice."

—Steve Jobs

*"To dream anything you want to dream—
that is the beauty of the human mind.
To do anything you want to do—
that is the strength of the human will.
To trust yourself to test your limits—
that is the courage to succeed."*

—Bernard Edwards

"The cave you fear to enter holds the treasure you seek."

—Joseph Campbell

"There are no guarantees. From the viewpoint of fear, none are strong enough. From the viewpoint of love, none are necessary."

—Emmanuel

"Those who can't see it for themselves, can't see it for you, either."

—Les Brown

"Follow your bliss and the Universe will open doors for you where there were only walls."

—Joseph Campbell

"It had long since come to my attention that people of accomplishment rarely sat back and let things happen to them. They went out and happened to things."
—Eleanor Furneaux Smith

"You're special and unique among all the creatures on the planet earth. You've been endowed with the capacity and the power to create desirable pictures inside your mind and to find them automatically printed in the outer world of your environment. All your dreams can come true, if you have the courage to pursue them."
—The Daily Guru

"You can't solve a problem with the same thinking that created it."
—Albert Einstein

"If you have built castles in the air, your work need not be lost; that is where they should be. Now put foundations under them."
—Henry David Thoreau

"To be free is to have achieved your life."
—Tennessee Williams

"No matter what our achievements might be, we think well of ourselves only in rare moments. We need people to bear witness against our inner judge, who keeps book on our shortcomings and transgressions. We need people to convince us that we are not as bad as we think we are."
—Eric Hoffer

"The signs of the zodiac are karmic patterns; the planets are the looms; the will is the weaver."
—Anonymous

"It's the action, not the fruit of the action, that's important. You have to do the right thing. It may not be in your power, may not be in your time, that there'll be any fruit. But that doesn't mean you stop doing the right thing. You may never know what results come from your action. But if you do nothing, there will be no result."
—Mahatma Gandhi

"How to get rid of ego as dictator and turn it into messenger and servant and scout, to be in your service, is the trick."
—Joseph Campbell

"Half of our mistakes in life stem from feeling where we ought to think, and thinking where we ought to feel."
—John Churton Collins

"The creative act is not hanging on, but yielding to a new creative movement. Awe is what moves us forward."
—Joseph Campbell

"Action may not always bring happiness, but there is no happiness without action."
—Benjamin Disraeli

"You don't have to be great to start, but you do have to start to be great."
—Zig Ziglar

"It takes as much energy to wish as it does to plan."
—Eleanor Roosevelt

"To finish first you must first finish."
—Rick Mears

"Success is not a secret; it is a system."
—Florence Scovel Shinn

"Unless it is supported by a practical plan, no creative, mundane or spiritual concept can come to successful fruition."
—Sheilaa Hite

"Those who see the invisible can do the impossible."
—Pandurang Shastri Vaijnath Athavale

"It always seems impossible until it's done."
—Nelson Mandela

"While they were saying among themselves it cannot be done, it was done."
—Helen Keller

"For we have not even to risk the adventure alone, for the heroes of all time have gone before us..."
—Joseph Campbell

"Dream lofty dreams, and as you dream, so you shall become. Your vision is the promise of what you shall one day be;   your ideal is the prophecy of what you shall at last unveil."
—James Allen

"Whatever you do, you need courage. Whatever course you decide upon, there is always someone to tell you you are wrong. There are always difficulties arising which tempt you to believe that your critics are right. To map out a course of action and follow it to the end, requires some of the same courage which a soldier needs."
—Ralph Waldo Emerson

"It is a terrible thing to see and have no vision."
—Helen Keller

"It's not the size of the dog in the fight, it's the size of the fight in the dog."
—Mark Twain

"That which we persist in doing becomes easier, not that the task itself has become easier, but that our ability to perform it has improved."
—Ralph Waldo Emerson

"You are free to believe what you choose and what you do attests to what you believe."
—A Course of Miracles

"Discovery consists in seeing what everyone else has seen   and thinking what no one else has thought."
—Albert Szent-Gyorgyi

Whatever you do, you need courage. Whatever course you decide upon, there is always someone to tell you you are wrong. There are always difficulties arising which tempt you to believe that your critics are right. To map out a course of action and follow it to the end, requires some of the same courage which a soldier needs."
—Ralph Waldo Emerson

"Follow your bliss. If you do follow your bliss, you put yourself on a kind of track that has been there all the while waiting for you, and the life you ought to be living is the one you are living. When you can see that, you begin to meet people who are in the field of your bliss, and they open the doors to you. I say, follow your bliss and don't be afraid, and doors will open where you didn't know they were going to be. If you follow your bliss, doors will open for you that wouldn't have opened for anyone else."
—Joseph Campbell

"Commitment is what transforms a promise into reality. It is the words that speak boldly of your intentions. And the actions which speak louder than the words. It is making the time when there is none. Coming through time after time after time, year after year after year. Commitment is the stuff character is made of; the power to change the face of things. It is the daily triumph of integrity over skepticism."
—Abraham Lincoln

"The character of greatness must be measured in two ways, else the measurement is flawed. First, is by one's ability to succeed in times of trial where others may fail. Secondly, and perhaps foundational to any form of greatness, is one's willingness to start over in spite of failure, when success seems farthest away."
—The Daily Guru

"At first people refuse to believe that a strange new thing can be done. Then they begin to hope it can be done. Then they see it can be done. Then it is done and all the world wonders why it was not done centuries ago."
—Frances Hodgson Burnett

*"Until one is committed, there is hesitancy, the chance
to draw back, always ineffectiveness. Concerning all acts
of initiative (and creation) there is one elementary truth—
the ignorance of which kills countless ideas and splendid plans—
the moment one definitely commits oneself, then Providence
moves too. All sorts of things occur to help
one that would never otherwise have occurred. A whole system of
events issues from the decision—raising in one's favor all manner
of unforeseen incidents and meetings
and material assistance—which no one could have ever dreamed
would have come one's way. I have learned a
deep respect for one of Goethe's couplets:
'Whatever you can do, or dream you can~
begin it now.
Boldness has genius, power and magic in it.'"*
—William Hutchinson Murray

*"Any task can be accomplished if it's broken down into
manageable parts."*
—Universal Truth

*"Never confuse someone else's inability to do something with its
inability to be done."*
—Steve Maraboli

"One monkey don't stop no show!"
—Big Maybelle

*"You don't have to be a fantastic hero to do certain things—to
compete. You can be just an ordinary chap, sufficiently
motivated."*
—Sir Edmund Hillary

"Do what you do and do it good."
—Q

*"The pessimist sees the difficulty in every opportunity;
the optimist, the opportunity in every difficulty."*
—L. P. Jacks

"Never be afraid to try something new. Remember, amateurs built the ark. Professionals built the Titanic."
—Charles M. Schulz

"When a defining moment comes along, you define the moment, or the moment defines you."
—Film, "The Tin Cup"

"Take care to get what you like or you will be forced to like what you get."
—George Bernard Shaw

"Suit the action to the word, the word to the action."
—William Shakespeare

"Words are also actions, and actions are a kind of words."
—Ralph Waldo Emerson

"Do not wait to strike till the iron is hot; but make it hot by striking."
—William B. Sprague

"It's better to be prepared for an opportunity that never happens, than to be unprepared for one that does."
—Les Brown

"Winners never quit and quitters never win."
—Anonymous

"The way we see the problem is often the problem."
—Stephen Covey

"Failing to prepare is preparing to fail."
—Coach John Wooden

"There are those who look at things the way they are, and ask 'why?'... I dream of things that never were, and ask 'why not?'"
—Robert F. Kennedy

"Faced with the choice between changing one's mind and proving that there is no need to do so, almost everyone gets busy on the proof."
—John Kenneth Galbraith

"The question is not what you look at, but what you see."
—Henry David Thoreau

"The first step to completing an overwhelming task is to complete the first step."
—Anonymous

"Great things are not done by impulse, but by a series of small things brought together."
—Vincent Van Gogh

"Our grand business in life is not to see what lies dimly at a distance, but to do what lies clearly at hand."
—Thomas Carlyle

"There are painters who transform the sun into a yellow spot, but there are others who, thanks to their art and intelligence, transform a yellow spot into the sun."
—Pablo Picasso

"When the going gets tough, the tough get going."
(when situations are difficult, strong people rise to the occasion)
—Anonymous

"If you want to build a ship, don't drum up the people to gather wood, divide the work, and give orders. Instead, teach them to yearn of the vast and endless sea."
—Antoine de Saint Exupery

To paraphrase Samuel Johnson,
"The two most engaging powers of an innovator are to make new things familiar, and familiar things new."
—Samuel Johnson

194

"The reasonable man adapts himself to the world; the unreasonable one persists to adapt the world to himself. Therefore all progress depends on the unreasonable man."
—George Bernard Shaw

"Each success brings with it the potential of failure and each failure brings with it the potential of success."
—John F. Kennedy

"Remember that failure is an event, not a person."
—Zig Ziglar

"The power to move the world is in the subconscious mind."
—William James

"Whether you think you can or think you can't, you're right."
—Henry Ford

"The intuitive mind is a sacred gift. And the rational mind is a faithful servant. We have created a society that honors the servant and has forgotten the gift."
—Albert Einstein

"Don't wait. The time will never be just right."
—Napoleon Hill

"It's a step at a time...and these are the steps."
—Sheilaa Hite

"Our habits form our future."
—Anonymous

"A goal is a dream with a deadline."
—Napoleon Hill

"Become a possibilitarian. No matter how dark things seem to be or actually are, raise your sights and see possibilities—always see them, for they're always there."
—Dr. Norman Vincent Peale

"I have the simplest tastes. I am always satisfied with the best."
—Oscar Wilde

"One of the saddest lines in the world is, 'Oh come now—be realistic.' The best parts of this world were not fashioned by those who were realistic. They were fashioned by those who dared to look hard at their wishes and gave them horses to ride."
—Richard Nelson Bolles

"The world would have you agree with its dismal dream of limitation. But the Light would have you soar like the eagle of your sacred visions."
—Alan Cohen

"A goal without a plan is just a wish."
—Antoine de Saint-Exupery

"And those who were seen dancing were thought to be insane by those who could not hear the music."
—Angela Monet

"What you get by achieving your goals is not as important as what you become by achieving your goals."
—Zig Zigler

"Every great work, every big accomplishment, has been brought into manifestation through holding to the vision, and often just before the big achievement, comes apparent failure and discouragement."
—Florence Scovel Shinn

"Half of our mistakes in life stem from feeling where we ought to think, and thinking where we ought to feel."
—John Churton Collins

"Commitment is doing the thing you said you'd do, long after the mood you said it in has left you!"
—Georg Zalucki

"Commitment is healthiest when it is not without doubt but in spite of doubt."

—Rollo May

"It's not our mistakes that define us, it's what we do afterwards that counts."

—Anonymous

"If I had asked people what they wanted, they would have said faster horses."

—Henry Ford

"You say I started out with practically nothing, but that isn't correct. We all start with all there is, it's how we use it that makes things possible."

—Henry Ford

"People with high levels of personal mastery do not set out to integrate reason and intuition. Rather, they achieve it naturally—as a by-product of their commitment to use all the resources at their disposal. They cannot afford to choose between reason and intuition, or head and heart, any more than they would choose to walk on one leg or see with one eye."

—Peter Senge

"Life is a series of experiences, each of which makes us bigger, even though it is hard to realize this. For the world was built to develop character, and we must learn that the setbacks and griefs which we endure help us in our marching onward."

—Henry Ford

"Don't find fault, find a remedy; anybody can complain."

—Henry Ford

I am looking for a lot of men who have an infinite capacity to <u>not</u> know what can't be done.

—Henry Ford

"Vision without execution is just hallucination."
—Henry Ford

"I have not failed.
I've just found 10,000 ways that won't work."
—Thomas Alva Edison

"Notice the difference between what happens when a person says to themselves, 'I have failed three times,' and what happens when they say, 'I am a failure.'"
—S.I. Hayakawa

"We do not truly serve the world if we give to others but neglect our own truth and our own needs. It's only when our own needs are fully met that we can generously and whole-heartedly give of ourselves. It's not selfish to look after ourselves—it's essential."
—Pearl S. Buck

"You can decide to alter the course of your life at any time. No one can ever take that away from you. You can decide what you want and go after it. It's always your next move."
—Various Authors

"The, only limits are as always, those of vision."
—James Broughton

"Whatever it takes—ignore people who say it can't be done."
—Elaine Rideout

"Life is a banquet and most poor suckers are starving to death."
—"Auntie Mame" Dennis

"For all sad words of tongue and pen, the saddest are these—
'It might have been.'"
—John Greenleaf Whittier

"Two roads diverged in a wood, and I...
I took the one less traveled by
—and that has made all the difference."
—Robert Frost

*"If you want to build a ship, don't drum up the people
to gather wood, divide the work, and give orders.
Instead, teach them to yearn of the vast and endless sea."*
—Antoine de Saint Exupery

*"When it is obvious that the goals cannot be reached,
don't adjust the goals, adjust the action steps."*
—Confucius

*"If your actions inspire others to dream more, learn more, do
more and become more, you are a leader."*
—John Quincy Adams

*"When you let intuition have its way with you,
you open up new levels of the world. Such
opening-up is the most practical of all activities."*
—Evelyn Underhill

"Nothing in the world can take the place of persistence.
Talent will not—*nothing is more common than unsuccessful men
with talent.* Genius will not—u*nrewarded genius is almost a
proverb.* Education will not—*the world is full of educated
derelicts.* Persistence, Determination and Faith alone are
omnipotent.*"*
—Calvin Coolidge

*"...Our deepest fear is not that we are inadequate.
Our deepest fear is that we are powerful beyond measure.
It is our light, not our darkness, that most frightens us.
We ask ourselves, who am I to be brilliant, gorgeous, talented,
fabulous? Actually, who are you not to be? You are a child of God.
Your playing small doesn't serve the world. There's nothing
enlightened about shrinking so that other people won't feel
insecure around you. We are all meant to shine, as children do.
We were born to make manifest the glory of God that is within
us. It's not just in some of us; it's in everyone. And as we let our
own light shine, we unconsciously give other people permission to
do the same. As we're liberated from our own fear, our presence
automatically liberates others."*
—Marianne Williamson

"I learned this, at least, by my experiment: that if one advances confidently in the direction of his dreams, and endeavors to live the life which he has imagined, he will meet with a success unexpected in common hours.
He will put some things behind, will pass an invisible boundary; new, universal, and more liberal laws will begin to establish themselves around and within him; or the old laws be expanded, and interpreted in his favor in a more liberal sense, and he will live with the license of a higher order of beings. In proportion, as he simplifies his life, the laws of the universe will appear less complex, and solitude will not be solitude, nor poverty poverty, nor weakness weakness.
If you have built castles in the air, your work need not be lost; that is where they should be. Now put the foundations under them."

—Henry David Thoreau

"It's kind of fun to do the impossible."

—Walt Disney

"All human creativity begins with imagination and with a willingness to consider the possibility that something heretofore unimagined might actually come into being.
Let go of limiting assumptions, and an Infinite universe will instantly manifest— right before your very eyes."

—Daily Guru

"To risk is to risk appearing the fool. To weep is to risk appearing sentimental. To expose feelings is to risk exposing your true self. To place your ideas, your dreams before the crowd is to risk loss. To love is to risk not being loved in return. To live is to risk dying. To try at all is to risk failure.
But to risk we must. Because the greatest hazard in life is to risk nothing. The man, the woman, who risks nothing, does nothing, has nothing, is nothing."

—Ralph Waldo Emerson

\

"Me—On Being Great"©

"People have called me intense all my life. I have always been mystified by what they meant by that word—intense. There always seemed to be an implication of abnormality whenever they referred to me that way.

I am me—this is how it is for me. I am normal the way I am. This is normal; this is me.

Yes, I am intense and it is perfectly normal for me to be intense, thank God! Yes, I am also powerful. I was born this way. Power and I are the same. We Are by design of God, the Creator.

Every instant of my life, I dance on the point of the flame of all existence. Every hour, every minute, every second of my life—I die and am reborn. The pyre is the center point of my being. I am always either descending into the flames, being consumed by them, dying; or I am the Phoenix, rising from the ashes, to live again the cycle of birth, death, rebirth = the Cycle of Transformation.

This is immortality; this is what immortality is. Immortality doesn't mean never dying. Immortality means dying, being reborn, dying, being reborn, endlessly into and beyond infinity. We are all immortal; how could we not be? I Am immortal. Immortality is the cycle of life and that cycle cannot be broken.

I own my power, my intensity, my Greatness. I am finally able to. I own it, I claim it. Because I claim it, I am invincible. My strength and power are one with God—for God is the pyre, the flame, the ashes, the Phoenix, the Dance—and so am I.

I live in the center of it, I always have. Now I am conscious of my home, my heart, my heritage, my worth, my wealth—and I claim them. With my consciousness and my claim, comes my understanding and acceptance of my meaning, my life, my life force—myself.

With my understanding and acceptance, comes My Mastery... and with mastery, there is no longer mystery; there is only certainty.

I no longer doubt. The Greatness I am, already is, always has been. I no longer fret about my ascendancy, does the Sun fret, or does the Sun know? It is only a matter of time.
All I have to do is be me, and that is easy—I can do nothing else."

—Sheilaa Hite

Mentors, Life Coaches, Support Groups
and Social Media Sites

Mentors

Members of mentoring programs are matched with individuals possessing the appropriate skills and desires to ensure a successful mentor/mentee relationship. Mentoring programs are as varied as the organizations that sponsor them; here are a few.

S.C.O.R.E., Service Corps of Retired Executives – www.score.org. They have a great reputation and a high success rate of their mentees achieving their goals.

Peer Resources and Mentor Programs
http://www.peer.ca/mentorprograms.html
A very comprehensive catalog of all types of mentors for all types of people. Scroll down to the MENTOR PROGRAM AND SERVICE CHARACTERISTICS section and click on the categories that interest you.

The Impact Center - http://www.the-impact-center.org
A women's mentoring organization based in Washington, DC.

Life Coaches

Sheilaa Hite, CLC, C.ht – www.SheilaaHite.com.
For information about me, go to my website, as well as read the Introduction at the beginning of the book and read the Testimonials and About the Author chapters at the back of the book.

There is a Life Coach for just about anything you can think of. I recommend you google "life coaches" for a comprehensive list. Choose the one who best fits you and your vision.

Support Groups

Just as with Life Coaches, there are support groups who specialize in a variety of fields.

To find one that meets your criterion, google "support groups" and choose the group that best fits you and your vision.

Social Media Sites

Facebook – www.facebook.com

Twitter – www.twitter.com

LinkedIn – www.linkedin.com

The Pictorial Muses

The Three Pictorial Muse Images that will describe you and your quest

Image 1 -

_____
_____
_____
_____
_____
_____
_____

Image 2 -

_____
_____
_____
_____
_____
_____
_____

Image 3 -

_____
_____
_____
_____
_____
_____
_____

The Four Pictorial Muse Images that'll identify the key energy of each stage

Image 1 – Stage 1

_____
_____
_____
_____
_____
_____
_____

Image 2 – Stage 2

_____
_____
_____
_____
_____
_____

Image 3 – Stage 3

_____
_____
_____
_____
_____
_____

Image 4 – Stage 4

_____
_____
_____
_____
_____
_____

Your Daily Pictorial Muse Image

Day _____ *Date* _____

Image _____
_____
_____
_____
_____
_____
_____
_____

Day _____ *Date* _____

Image _____
_____
_____
_____
_____
_____
_____
_____

Day _____ *Date* _____

Image _____
_____
_____
_____
_____
_____
_____
_____

Day _____ *Date* _____

Image _____

_____
_____
_____
_____
_____
_____
_____

Day _____ *Date* _____

Image _____

_____
_____
_____
_____
_____
_____
_____

Day _____ *Date* _____

Image _____

_____
_____
_____
_____
_____
_____
_____

Making Your Treasure Map

1- Decide what you want: what qualities you need, what circumstances you want, what you want to become, what you want to have, what you want to do, what you are grateful for.

2- Clip words, titles, and pictures from magazines, newspapers, and/or catalogs that represent your vision of how you want your life to be as a result of using this system. You can also print out affirmations and use those. Make sure you have a photo of yourself, too.

3- On a sheet of poster board or foam core, 22"x28" is a good size, paste your clippings on it. Start by putting your photo in the center of the board (like the Sun in the Universe) and paste your clippings around it in an uncluttered pattern that pleases you. It generally takes 1-3 days to make one.

4- Put your treasure map in a place where you can see it, but not in a high traffic area where others might criticize you or cast doubt on you achieving your goal. If you have to keep it covered or put away from others sometimes, that's OK, do take it out and look at it on a regular basis, though, if that's the case.

5- Look at or "read" your map at least once a day and visualize or imagine yourself living the life it depicts. Often, ideas will come to you as you look at your map. Those ideas are intuitive messages and I recommend that you write them down and follow up on them.

6- If your current map no longer correctly reflects you and your desired vision, make a new map. If that becomes the case, you've outgrown the old one and will benefit from a more accurate visual reminder.

7- It's important that your map reflects what you really want. Please don't ask for something less than what you want.

Creating this map is your opportunity to place your order with the Universe—Go For It!

8- Place the phrase, *"Thank You,"* under your photo at the map's center.

"Living Inspiration"—the rest of the story...

From Chapter 4 – My Guided Imagery CD's

When faced with the fact that my original vision of the singular goal of putting together an appealing proposal package to get funding for my guided imagery meditations: sheets of paper with tantalizing information on them in an attractive presentation folder had, in only a few days, led to an opportunity to affordably record, reproduce, package and distribute my CD's, I felt like I was in another dimension. Things had moved so quickly and in such a different direction that I almost wanted to shout to the Universe, *"Wait, I have a plan and a schedule here, what about them!?"*

I didn't though. Instead, I centered and grounded myself, thanked God for my luck and went in the new direction. The recording session went well and the reproduction facility and packaging company lived up to the producer's recommendations. Since I didn't have the original artwork I wanted for the covers, I used my photograph, instead.

When I picked up the finished, packaged CD's from the packager, I was so stoked! I couldn't wait to tell my class at the next session how well the system was working for me.

Late that night, I was sitting at home going over my original Commitment statement and "Steps Necessary to Complete My Goal" instruction guide and reflecting on the whirlwind series of events I'd just experienced and thought that the only things I hadn't nailed down were international distributorship and artwork for the CD covers.

I was feeling pretty good about myself when the phone rang. The caller was the owner of a metaphysical shop in London that I'd worked in when I lived there. *"I hope I'm not calling too late; it's morning here,"* he said by way of greeting. I like to stay up late and I assured him it wasn't too late for me. *"I have an·idea, why don't you come over for six weeks and work in my shop again. We can arrange for you to take a group of people to Avebury and Stonehenge, too. Your old clients are chuffed at the idea of seeing you again and I've got new clients already lined up for you, too."*

I'd been wanting to visit London again, but I was too busy with other projects to arrange a trip. Of course I said, *"Yes."* We talked a bit more and I told him about my CD's. He offered to sell them in his shop and promised to help me distribute them in other UK cities. Once again, I thanked God for my luck and thought, *"the only task remaining now is to find an artist and commission the cover art for the CD's,"* when he said, *"My friend Helen wants a consultation with you, too, but she's broke. She's a painter and was wondering if you'd be interested in trading a consultation for some of her artwork."*

There was a long pause. I couldn't say anything, and he must have thought the call had been dropped because I remember hearing him say, *"Hello, hello–are you still there?"* After a few seconds, I was able to reply that I was and that I was definitely interested in talking to Helen about her offer. We discussed the details for my London stay and then we rang off.

Whew! I sat in my living room in a daze. I hadn't even verbalized my requests and in a few minutes they'd all been granted. This manifestation system was intense—I'd just been given convincing proof of it and it was powerful stuff!

At the next class session, I began the class by announcing to my students that the manifestation system wasn't working the way I'd originally thought, so I wasn't going to continue with my project of putting a presentation package together for prospective investors.

They looked confused and some of them asked what had happened to make me change my mind, especially since I'd been so enthusiastic about the system and my presentation project. *"Don't you still want the investors?"* one of them asked. I ended their agony by announcing that I didn't need the presentation package anymore, as I held up my hands with the CD's in them, because, *"the manifestation system took its own course and I now have the actual CD's and everything on my Commitment Statement, including the artwork and an international distributor."*

They looked at the CD's, then they looked at me, then they looked at the CD's again. This went on for a couple of minutes. I could tell that they had no frame of reference for processing what I'd just told and shown them. Finally their thought processes caught up with real time and they burst into applause and cheers. If any of them had previously doubted the efficacy of the manifestation system, the doubt was gone now.

I call occurrences like that, "powerful demonstrations." Everyone in that class witnessed my "powerful demonstration" and was highly motivated to keep working on manifesting their vision and experiencing their own "powerful demonstration." Every one of my students "came through," too. They all continued to work the manifestation system and they all achieved their goals in spectacular fashion.

A few weeks later, in London, Helen and I met and, of course I liked her artwork; I knew I would. Everything had been so perfectly laid out for me; how could I not like it.

From Chapter 5 – Abby and Her Financial Quest

Abby's decision to learn about finance and investment so that she could wrest control of her family's stock portfolio from their current money manager and manage it herself was a real game changer for her, her family and eventually her friends.

When she'd first announced that she was going to make that her class manifestation project, I was nervous and concerned for her. I didn't let that get in the way of encouraging or supporting her, though. I intuitively knew that regardless of the outcome, she'd be a better person because of her experience in pursuing such a challenging quest.

At our next class session, Abby enthralled us with her report of her activities and experiences during the week between classes. She spoke about magic and luck and something we referred to in the ashram I lived in for a time in India as, "Prasad," which means, the blessed gift of the Divine.

The morning following the previous week's class, she came across a full page ad in the Times, announcing that a new six week course was being offered to teach people how to personally manage their financial portfolios. She signed up for the course immediately. When she went to the library to find books on the subject, she found out that the reference librarian had a background in investment portfolios and had just been waiting for someone, anyone, to ask her for any information about it. She and the librarian hit it off and a mentor-mentee relationship was formed between the two of them. Her new mentor still had contacts in the investment world and began arranging for Abby to meet with various experts so that she could "pick their brains."

The new arena she'd just entered and the speed with which everything was happening, was all still very new and somewhat dizzying to her. She still had to attend to the needs of her home and family, so she was also challenged with how to make her new interest and her old life mesh.

As the weeks went on, her intellectual skills and strong will, along with her fierce determination, really helped her as she navigated the intricate channels of the financial mindset. I noticed that she was changing, too. Pretty and always stylishly dressed, her look was becoming sharper and more defined. She exuded a higher level of self-confidence, too, with each financial investment class session she attended and with each meeting she took with a financial expert.

When the six week financial investment course was finished, so was our first round of manifestation classes. Our class took a two week break, but Abby didn't. She found another financial planning class and kept studying. Three months after beginning her work with the manifestation system, she announced to the class that she'd finally convinced her husband to let her take over their stock portfolio. He'd been skeptical at first but he'd become convinced that she knew what she was doing when she accurately predicted the market's trends and the reasons for them over a three week period.

Abby was like a determined knight on a bold and dangerous quest and we looked forward to hearing about her latest exploits each week. It took her several more weeks to pry the money manager's hands from her family's portfolio. As she told us about these skirmishes with the misogynistic manager, we could all envision her in armor, riding into battle on a trusty steed and courageously fighting for her family's security. The night she came to class and announced that she'd finally won the battle and was now in control of her family's finances, we all cheered.

In managing the portfolio, she'd discovered proof that confirmed her feelings that she'd been right about her misgivings regarding the former money manager's handling of their finances. He wasn't dishonest, just inept. Under her watchful eye, their portfolio grew exponentially and she and her family prospered.

She didn't stop there. With her new-found expertise, she guided many of her friends to financial stability and helped save one of her neighbor's homes from foreclosure because of the fallout from a bad investment.

When the company her husband worked for wanted to relocate them again, she decided she didn't want to move. She convinced her husband to take an early retirement and he was able to negotiate a very nice retirement package. Before he signed off on it, she looked at it and told him, "*You worked for that company for years. You should have a better retirement package. Let me negotiate it for you.*" He'd learned to trust her financial advice, so they arranged a meeting with company heads.

Abby told me that when she walked into the conference room for the meeting and told the company heads that she'd be negotiating her husband's retirement package, they smirked. By the time the meeting ended, she'd negotiated a package that was three times greater than his original package!

Abby is one of my personal heroes. Of all of the people I've guided through this process, her transformation is the one that touches me the most. She's one of the reasons I love what I do.

From Chapter 7 – Bria and Her Executive Women's Retreat

When Bria first realized that her desire to create an off-the-beaten path retreat for executive women stemmed from her need and desire to get away from the pressures of her own hectic life and be attended to by others who were solicitous of and responding to her needs instead of the other way around, she positioned herself and her quest so that she could make that happen.

After getting almost half-way through the process that would lead to her getting her certification and making her dream a reality, she had a moment of brilliant insight. Even though she was calling her new goal an executive women's retreat, she was still going to be a yenta, only now she'd be her retreat client's yenta. By creating and hosting the retreat, she'd still be at everyone's beck and call and would wind up exactly where she was now; stressed and with her needs unattended.

That wasn't what she really wanted. So she stopped the planning and the certification process and did for herself what she'd done for so many others; she arranged for a two week stay at a mountain resort that boasted about it's no cell phone and internet policy. There, she was massaged and pampered and treated the way she treated everyone who came to her for help; with a sense of dedication and nurturing that told her that she mattered and her emotional, spiritual, mental and physical well-being were important to those who attended her.

Being treated this way was a first for Bria and she had to get used to having things done for her instead of doing for others. She realized that just as the people she took care of needed her, she needed them, too. Her identity was closely tied to the belief that if she wasn't helping someone, she wasn't being useful. When the maid gently chided her for doing something she hadn't been aware she was doing, helping the maid make the bed in her mountain resort hotel room, she knew she had to change the way she thought and take a different approach to herself and her life.

Bit-by-bit, she surrendered to being a guest and not a host. At the end of her two-week stay, she couldn't say that she'd had a restful time at the resort, but she did know that she'd had an insightful, transformational awakening while she was there.

Determined to keep the momentum going on her new path, she enrolled in a self-awareness workshop and began turning her cell phone off after 10pm each evening. It wasn't easy and she had to fight for it, but she learned to make space in her life for herself.

She is by nature and nurture a caretaker, and will always have to monitor herself to make sure she's being nurtured by herself and by those in her life to whom she gives so much. She's decided to go to the mountain retreat at least twice a year in order to stay balanced and in touch with herself and her needs. Calmer, more reflective and more at peace with herself these days, she's thinking of writing a book about her discovery of and journey back to herself.

Dave & Edward's Island Dream

Frustrated by their inability to obtain the necessary permits they needed to start their business, the twins approached their friend, Leia, and asked for her advice. Telling them she needed time to think about their problem, she invited them to assist her as she helped prepare for the island's annual harvest celebration. While spending time with their friend and helping the islanders with the harvest celebration preparations, they realized that they'd been disrespectful of the islanders, their traditions and the land by not learning about or acknowledging the importance of the island's history and traditional ceremonies. Although they were aware of the ceremonies, they, like most of the other foreigners who visited the island had considered these important traditions colorful, quaint, "native" practices.

By becoming involved with the preparations, they began to feel a real connection to the island and the people who lived there. The islanders noticed their genuine, heartfelt participation and accepted them into their community, which had been Leia's plan all along.

The following Monday, when the twins went to the island's city hall to again apply for their permits, they were greeted like family, with hugs and heartfelt warmth instead of the usual handshakes and formalities. When they left that meeting they had a real sense of belonging; they also had their permits.

With permits in hand, they opened their charter fishing business and dive shop. Their learning curve was steep, but after a few months, their advertising, appearances at the travel industry trade shows, personal service and ability to provide a unique experience started to pay off for them and their business began to flourish. So much so, that they're already getting high ratings from the top travel magazines and an article is being written about them by a travel writer for a major newspaper.

The experience of becoming part of the island community shifted their perspective and instead of wanting to just build a hotel for upscale tourists, they're now working on plans with the island officials to build a lodging retreat that offers a meaningful, mutually beneficial, interactive island experience for their guests and the islanders.

From Chapter 8 – Beverly's Dilemma

Beverly's a very talented artist, but her unwillingness to engage with all of the aspects of the creative process cost her dearly. She liked the first stages of creativity: the part where she was inspired and she could make plans to enter into a creative relationship with her muse and produce something that spoke of her inner self and her relationship with her deep connection to the soul of humanity. It was dealing with the actual challenges that always present themselves whenever a relationship with one's muse looms on the horizon that Beverly didn't like and was committed to avoiding at all costs.

But avoiding dealing with that part of the creative process was taking a toll on her and the effects of that high price were beginning to show up in her life big time. She became more and more irritable and began acting out from that space, thus becoming less pleasant to be around. Her stable, loving relationship with her boyfriend of six years was staring to fall apart because she'd descended into a type of neurotic neediness where she expected him to fill all of her emotional needs. And like a bottomless jug, she was never satisfied and always demanded more from him.

These changes in her life and relationships were all happening because she was blocking the channel for her strong, vital force of creative expression and, as we all know, much like tying a knot in a garden hose, when you stifle the flow of energy at its intended outlet, it'll find another, less predictable and often destructive outlet. Beverly's resistance to wholly engage with the creative process because she was trying to avoid the challenges, pains and obstacles that are also a part of creativity, was interpreted as a form of denial by her heart and soul. And the heart and soul don't deal well with being denied, they'll find their own channel of expression, no matter what the cost.

Beverly's tipping point came one afternoon when she was out walking through the park with a friend. Instead of seeing the beautiful surroundings and the beauty of her friendship, all she could focus on was the way life was betraying her by causing her so much unhappiness. Naturally, she felt it was her right to vigorously express her dissatisfaction and rain on everyone else's parade. Finally, her friend had had enough. She turned to her and said, *"Beverly, I want you to know I love you and because I love you, I'm going to tell you the truth about yourself to your face."* And she did.

Shocked and with a wounded ego, she equated this act of courageous love as a personal attack and ran off, vowing to never, ever speak to her friend again. As she sat alone in the park, she cried about being the victim of what she perceived as the cruelty and insensitivity of all of the people in her life who claimed to love her. She became so caught up in her drama that she imagined them all around her and actually shook her finger at them as she told the imaginary gathering off!

It was then, when she saw her finger pointing away from her that she recalled something her beloved grandmother used to say, *"Remember, when you point your finger at someone, three more are pointed back at you."*

Sitting alone in the park that afternoon was a metaphor for what she'd done to herself and her life. In the midst of all of the natural beauty, joy and love surrounding her, all she could focus on was how awful things were for her.

Soul searching is rarely a fun activity but it is a beneficial one and Beverly finally realized she needed to do it. She was frustrated and unhappy, her boyfriend was on the verge of leaving and her friends were keeping their distance. Since she was the only person who was constant in all of those situations, she began to accept the fact that she might be the source of her unhappiness. In a rare moment of clarity, she admitted the truth to herself and knew that she needed to honestly look at what was happening to her and why.

Her first attempts at doing this weren't very successful because she had little experience in connecting with her whole self. A few days later, while doing Tai-Chi in the park with a group that regularly met for the meditative exercise, she found herself standing next to a woman whose energy was wonderfully centered and calming. After the practice ended she struck up a conversation with the woman and learned that she was a psychologist who mainly worked with artists to help them remove the creative blocks that were preventing them from fully expressing themselves and living meaningful, fulfilling lives.

Able to recognize this "chance" meeting as an answered prayer, Beverly now sees this therapist on a regular basis and is beginning to understand how her life became so unmanageable. Her relationship with her boyfriend sustained a lot of damage and continues to be rocky, but he still loves her and is willing to work with her on it. She has hopes that they'll get it back on the smooth, loving track it was once on. Most of her friends are still with her, although, in being honest with herself, she can understand why some of them are keeping their distance. Hopefully, with time, introspection and doing the hard work of coming to terms with the totality of being a full participant in life, she'll heal and welcome that part of herself that her heart and soul recognize and respond to.

From Chapter 9 – Marco's Restaurant

After Marco's "save" from almost having wrecked his dream, he had to admit that he was a very lucky fellow, indeed. He also had to admit that he was a very obstinate and at times, very willful fellow, too.

No matter, though. He was used to his luck supporting and occasionally rescuing him when he took one of those crazy chances that very fortunate people like to take because they innately know that somehow, everything is going to work out for them.

He and his new restaurant thrived. Of course they would; the food and service were great, the ambiance was hip and exciting, the view overlooking the bay was magical and Marco was, well, Marco. Tall, dark, handsome and with an Italian-Senegalese accent, he was charming beyond belief. A flirt with all of the women and a buddy to all of the men, people wanted to be around him and they knew they could be if they went to his restaurant. Both the bar and restaurant were always crowded and reservations had to be made weeks in advance if anyone had any hope of getting one of the stunning view tables.

He's now decided he wants to have his own cooking show on television. He'll be great at it if he can make it happen. He, his investors and his advisors are excited about the prospect of taking the brand he established with the restaurant out into the world via personal appearances, products and celebrity endorsements.

Will Marco's new venture be successful? Will he follow or disregard all of the steps in the manifestation system? Will he heed the advice of his advisors? No one knows, not even Marco. I'm sure, though, that whatever he chooses to do, he'll do it in the Marco style and always land on his feet.

From Chapter 10 – My Coat

As fine as all of the acknowledgement and the compliments were, wearing the coat on that trip to Florence showed me that I still needed to make a few adjustments in order to achieve perfection. I realized that a couple of the fasteners needed to be repositioned and the coat would hang better if I tacked (stitched) the exquisite lining to the shell of the coat at the hem. I don't know if anyone else noticed those flaws; I did though, and I made the needed changes and the coat and I are both happier for it.

The following year, with the necessary adjustments made to it, I wore the coat to Paris. On my last day there, I visited the Museum of Decorative Arts, which is housed in a wing of the Louvre. As I admired one of the exhibits, a woman approached me, introduced herself to me as a curator and said, *"Madame, I must speak to you about your coat."*

"Your coat is beautiful. Did you know," she continued, *"that the way your coat's lining just barely shows itself all the way around the outside of the coat is the way coats were designed and made during the Renaissance?"*

When I answered in the affirmative, she went on, *"And the decorative trim and the beading on the cuffs—this is exactly how they made their outer garments."* She then grabbed my arm and for the next fifteen minutes, she took me from painting to tapestry to painting, pointing out the clothing in them and how I had gotten the spirit of the era and the details right.

Finally, after walking around me again as she continued to assess the coat, my accessories and me, she asked where I'd gotten it. When I told her I'd made the coat and it had taken me three months she exclaimed, *"But of course, this is art!"*

We parted company and it was all I could do to stay in my body. I was light-headed from the meaning and intensity of that encounter and I had to sit down. I am an artist and to be in one of art's holy temples, the Louvre, and in fashion's holy city, Paris, and have my work recognized and acknowledged by one of the curators of this great center was more than a dream come true, it was an anointing. That encounter was the outward confirmation of the rightness of following the dictates of my soul and creative spirit which are my motivating forces.

Did I need that moment of sublime acknowledgement? Yes. Not to tell me that I'm creative and have a right to express my creativity, but to act as a mirror for the results of my experience and the path that I trod in getting there.

Testimonials

"Thank you for helping me. Your help has been invaluable as it has allowed me to shift my perspective and give time to making my dreams a reality in this actual world—doing the step by step reality based work necessary to produce results on the physical plane."
LORRAINE BLANK - ENTREPRENEUR
THE BERKSHIRES, MA

~   ~   ~

"At a time when everyone seems to be hanging up their 'psychic shingle,' Ms. Hite demonstrates how it should be done—professional, skilled and inspiring."
TED ANDREWS - BEST SELLING AUTHOR OF
'*ANIMAL SPEAK*' and '*HOW TO MEET AND
WORK WITH YOUR SPIRIT GUIDES*'

~   ~   ~

"Sheilaa Hite is a magical coach-teacher-guide.
Like modern-day alchemists, we learned how to turn fear into power, trials into revelations and dreams into triumphant reality."
PAUL COLEMAN - VISIONARY ARTIST - PARIS, FRANCE

~   ~   ~

"In the tradition of great Intuitive Teachers, Sheilaa Hite has a special place because of her particular gift for understanding and interpreting the buried inspirations and creative destinies of the artists she advises."
SAM CHRISTENSEN & KEN CORTLAND - THE SAM
CHRISTENSEN STUDIOS - N. HWD, CA

~   ~   ~

"Sheilaa took time out of her busy schedule while on a book tour to spend time with some foster care girls who utilize our services. They were tentative at first—quiet and not trusting, but as Sheilaa began sharing her life experiences with them, I could see them start to melt. They began sharing with Sheilaa as she asked them just the right questions. They were dealing with difficult situations: an often absent, drug abusing father; an alcoholic mother and the chaos that comes with these circumstances, as well as other forms of familial dysfunction. These weren't "normal teen problems" that most of us faced, but difficult, traumatic events that could place them in the path of success or failure. Sheilaa's mixture of life wisdom and heart helped them see that they had the strength to make the right decisions. After only an hour, the girls left the workshop with more confidence in themselves. I don't know how she did it, but the brief time we were all together with Sheilaa, I witnessed something amazing."
STEPHANIE LORIG - DIRECTOR, ART WITH HEART
SEATTLE, WA

~   ~   ~

"Upon experiencing Sheilaa's work and the results
that were achieved because of it—I said to her,
'Oh—now I know what you do—you set people free!'"
V. EDWARD SCOTT - HEALTH CARE ADMINISTRATOR
LONDON, U.K.

~   ~   ~

"I cannot recommend Sheilaa Hite's intuitive and consultant work highly enough. The past two years of my life have been transformative - she has led me from confusion to clarity, and to joy. Not only is she an inspiring therapist, she is also always great fun to be with."
WINSLOW ELIOT - AUTHOR & PUBLISHER

~   ~   ~

"As a scientist and engineer, I was drawn to Sheilaa Hite's coaching workshops because she is a natural catalyst—she helps you make positive, profitable, lasting changes. She is astute, absolutely professional and eloquent. Through her wisdom and unique insight, I was guided to re-discover valuable qualities that I'd overlooked in myself and to create new, practical tools that have enabled me to more effectively and easily achieve my goals and increase my company's bottom line. I encourage everyone who can to work with her; it's the best investment you'll ever make!"
DR. KARL G. SMITH, Ph.D – PRESIDENT, KGS CONSULTING
EUROPE - ASIA - UNITED STATES

~ ~ ~

"Sheilaa is a magically marvelous, gracefully audacious being with sharp vision, compassionate, supportive empathy and a great sense of humor. She is a wonderful role model. Her life dares us to declare our dreams and celebrate life as the gift it is meant to be."
EUNICE KINGSLEY, M.A., M.L.S. – POET –
SANTA BARBARA, CA

~ ~ ~

"As a frustrated actress who always wore black, my career felt as dark as my clothes. Through Sheilaa Hite's guidance, I discovered my true path—within a year of working with her, I'd written, produced, directed and performed in my multi-award winning first film, '*Through Riley's Eyes.*' Through my own eyes, Sheilaa taught me to clearly see and own my power as I continue to create and embrace my destiny. Her book, *Power Secrets*, is the next best thing to working with Sheilaa personally."
SUE TURNER-CRAY – AUTEUR of MULTI-AWARD WINNING FILM, *"THROUGH RILEY'S EYES"*

~ ~ ~

*"I guide man to the path of the Divine and guard him from the red wolf
and the snake. * I set in his mortal hand my heavenly sword and put on
him the breastplate of the gods. * I break the ignorant pride of human
minds and lead the thought to the infiniteness of the truth. * I rend man's
narrow and successful life, and force his sorrowful eyes to gaze at the sun—
that he may die to earth and live in his soul. * I know the goal. * I know
the secret route. * I've studied the map of the invisible worlds. * I am the
battle's head, the journey's star."* "Whenever I think of your essence,
Sheilaa, I think of these words from the eastern deity, Tara. Thank
you for being the TARA in my life."
JOAN KELLY - PRODUCER - TOLUCA LAKE, CA

~   ~   ~

"You're a natural, Sheilaa. You're so clear in your vision because
you operate at such a high vibration. You just listen and let the
information channel through you—that's why people want to be
around you."
ROBERT PAGE - ARTIST - MILAN, ITALY

~   ~   ~

"An adept teacher and Intuitive, Sheilaa Hite is also a person of
intelligence, wisdom and heart. At the same time that she assists
others in their quest for inner guidance and personal
empowerment, she has the courage to live in commitment and
obedience to her own inner guidance, which is a powerful lesson in
itself."
NICOLE ROBERTS , Esq. - ATTORNEY -
SAN FRANCISCO, CA

~   ~   ~

"'What a lost person needs is a map of the territory, with his own
position marked on it so he can see where he is in relation to
everything else.' You're a great mapmaker, Sheilaa. Thank you for
showing me how to find my way."
COLIN SAMUELS - WRITER

~   ~   ~

"On July 26, Sheilaa told me my boyfriend would propose to me 'on bended knee' before Thanksgiving. On November 3, he proposed to me—while he was on one knee!"
BETH-RAE - ACTRESS - ("P.S. - I ACCEPTED!")

~ ~ ~

"Sheilaa Hite is a great reader! Her ability to empathize with you as she delivers her very accurate insights with class and eloquence is such a gift. I'm always inspired whenever she reads for me. I love her and so does everyone else I recommend her to."
CARIELL LUSIGNAN - OWNER, CAROL'S RESTAURANT - LENOX, MA & SEDONA, AZ

~ ~ ~

"Sheilaa, These past couple of years have taught me many things, and I know I wouldn't be standing where I am today, had I not had your love, guidance and friendship. While I can't say that all is over or past me yet, or as I wish it to be, I am still standing, and that speaks volumes. As I celebrate my birthday this year, I wanted to do so by reaching out to you and requesting a reading. You have always been an instrumental guide and gift in my life, giving me clarity and courage when I was incapable and/or unwilling to give it to or see it myself. I am excited by this coming reading, not because "all will be revealed," because you and I know full well, how the "Front Office" works. More so, I am excited because it is an opportunity to reconnect to all that is truly important to me; you, God, the Universe and the message and gift of listening."
JAMES WECKER - DearJames.com - SPIRITUAL ADVISOR & LIFE COACH

~ ~ ~

"Sheilaa's light radiates with grace; her teachings radiate with clarity and power."
SAM ROSSI - MALIBU, CA

~ ~ ~

"Sheilaa is a 100% accurate reader and as my personal astrologer, her advice produced incredible insights and results for me; as a compassionate and wonderful teacher and in helping me realize my own intuitive skills, she opened up a whole new world for me that has deeply affected and altered every single aspect of my life. She is, quite simply—the best! (Sheilaa, you sure changed my life—I realized just how much I'm indebted to you when I started writing this testimonial!)"
DAVID NATHAN, INTERNATIONAL MUSIC JOURNALIST, PRODUCER - LONDON (UK)

~ ~ ~

"I've consulted with Sheilaa Hite for nearly 20 years. She has the unique ability of being able to combine spirituality and practicality as she reads for you. You will find her to be an asset to you. She was a huge draw for my shop (accounting for 25% of the shop's revenue), continually attracting new clients; many of whom became repeat clients who in turn referred new clients to her."
ELIZABETH SHAW - LENOX, MA

~ ~ ~

"When Sheilaa 'reads' for you, it's as if your Higher Guidance is speaking to you."
G. GRIFFIS - PRODUCER

~ ~ ~

"There are fakes, there are phonies and there is the real thing. Sheilaa Hite is the real thing! She helps you to accept and appreciate who you are and where you are now, as a result of your past experiences. She then gently helps you to release the past as she teaches you how to use your own personal power to enrich and empower yourself so that you can successfully and responsibly create and enjoy the life you want."
P. A., SINGER - LONDON, EUROPE, USA

~ ~ ~

"When I saw her photo, I trusted her immediately (and I am a very
skeptical person). I 'knew' that Sheilaa was the person to guide me
in finding myself and connecting with the love of the Creator.
Through her guidance, I am no longer a victim and I have a life I
am happy to live. She is 'spot-on'—her ancient wisdom is very
connected to a Divine Source and can transform every aspect of
your life. She is truly magical!"
ROZ TITERA - GRAPHIC DESIGNER - LONDON

~ ~ ~

"I have taken many metaphysical courses and have always left
feeling slightly disappointed. After spending a full day with Sheilaa
Hite, I left feeling not only satisfied, but happier, calmer and more
confident in my intuitive abilities. It was everything I hoped to
learn about the Tarot and so much more. I am so grateful for what
was an extraordinary day. Thank you Sheilaa!"
DEBORA CUMMINGS, COMMODITIES BROKER,
PHILADELPHIA, PA

~ ~ ~

"I attended your Tarot seminar because for the past ten years, I
have 'played' with Tarot cards, actually knowing very little about
them. As a teacher, I like how fair and open minded you are and I
appreciate how close a connection you have with God and faith, as
well as your gift of bringing hope, humor and understanding (and
whatever else you do!) to others. You presented a lot of very
complex material in a very efficient and understandable way to a
rather wide range of experienced and beginning students. You gave
me an excellent foundation and framework from which to build a
solid relationship with the Tarot. All in all, it was an energizing and
informative day!"
LAURIE MARCHESSAULT - ARTIST - NEW HAVEN, CT

~ ~ ~

"A few years ago I decided to make big changes in every facet of my life. With the practical tools, inspirations and insights I garnered from Sheilaa Hite's workshops and hypnotherapy sessions, those once daunting, seemingly impossible to attain goals have all been reached. Because Sheilaa is incredibly adept and sees that all things are possible, she helped me map and travel the invisible routes to my goals. Her optimism, skills, down-to-earth wisdom and unique approach to aligning the spirit with the mundane, have given me the confidence and courage I needed to go beyond even my wildest dreams!"
HELEN POWERS - NURSE PRACTITIONER
VANCOUVER, BC

~ ~ ~

"Although, I'd worked with the Tarot for three years, I didn't have the confidence to read for others. After spending one day with Sheilaa in her Tarot Master Class, I'm now ready to read for others. Sheilaa is one of the most engaging, outstanding teachers you'll ever have the privilege to learn from. Her energy makes you comfortable the minute you meet her. Though there were others in the classroom, she made me feel as if I was working one on one with her. She literally taught me how to read the cards in one day! She guided me to an entirely new level that I wasn't even aware that I was capable of. As a teacher, she's one of the best that you'll ever encounter. As a person, I can't even begin to say enough good about her. She sincerely cares about her students. I was truly blessed to have been in her presence that day and I look forward to taking more classes with her in the future."
BRANDY LATSHAW - WEBSITE DESIGNER
WESTFIELD, MA

~ ~ ~

"As I reflect on all the 'Magic and Miracles' I've experienced in my life, I am eternally grateful to that part of myself that knows when to listen carefully. If anyone is tapped into that frequency, Sheilaa, it's you! You are a beautiful example of that kind of listening. I love the way you have facilitated others in seeing, hearing, feeling, speaking and living their truth. I love you. Thank you for being."
IRENE CHEN STANLEY – PUBLISHER, UNICUS MAGAZINE
MANHATTAN BEACH, CA

~ ~ ~

About the Author

"What we are is God's gift to us—
what we become is our gift to God."
—Ralph Waldo Emerson

Acknowledged as original, charismatic and brilliantly insightful, Sheilaa Hite, CLC, C.Ht., is one of the foremost life-skills mentors alive today. As a catalyst of the soul and mind, her extraordinary ability to recognize, integrate and align the energies of the four creative realms have made her mastery at teaching others how to turn "lead into gold," legendary. By synthesizing the expertise of her lifetime, extensive practical experience, sharp business acumen, innate intelligence and spot-on intuition, she uniquely unites and ignites the key elements that help guide her clients and students as they learn the modern-day alchemy secrets of making their dreams come true.

An internationally acclaimed Life Coach, teacher, speaker, Board Certified Clinical Hypnotherapist, media consultant, author and Master of the Intuitive Arts, she has been featured on television in such programs as Entertainment Tonight, American Movie Classics, E! Television and NBC's groundbreaking, "The Other Side." Her international client list numbers in the thousands and includes TV, movie and sports celebrities, politicians, homemakers, business professionals and members of the clergy and military. Her articles and columns have also appeared on-line, as well as in numerous national and international publications. Through her company, Odysseys—Grand Travel Experiences for the Heart, Spirit, Body and Mind, she also conducts tours and leads retreats to beautiful, inspiring places throughout the world.

Made in the USA
Las Vegas, NV
13 October 2021